# HOW TO
# PLAY GUITAR

# HOW TO
# PLAY GUITAR

a new book for everyone interested in the guitar

## Roger Evans

Elm Tree Books
EMI Music Publishing

Copyright © 1979 by EMI Music Publishing Ltd

First published in Great Britain 1979
by Elm Tree Books Ltd
27 Wrights Lane, London W8 5TZ
in association with EMI Music Publishing Ltd
International Music Publications
Southend Road, Woodford Green, Essex IG8
8HN

14th Impression 1989

British Library Cataloguing in Publication Data
Evans, Roger
    How to play guitar.
    1. Guitar – Methods – Self-instruction
    I. Title
    787'.61'0712        MT588

        ISBN 0-241-10324-X
        ISBN 0-241-10323-1 Pbk

Printed in Great Britain by
St Edmundsbury Press Ltd,
Bury St Edmunds, Suffolk

# Contents

# Introduction

This new book is for everyone who is interested in playing the guitar. It is for the absolute beginner, and for those who already play.

For the beginner, everything is explained in simple easy-to-understand stages, so you can start to learn how to play the music of your choice— Pop, Folk, Country, Rock, Blues, Jazz, Classical and other styles. This book even explains how to learn to play if you are left-handed. You need have no knowledge of music or the guitar to start playing immediately and entertain yourself on the guitar.

For those who already play, there are numerous hints and 'tricks of the trade' normally known only to professional musicians with many years experience. Techniques of different styles of playing are explained simply, to help you become a better guitarist and get more enjoyment from your guitar playing.

How quickly you learn to play depends entirely on you. With this book, you can learn at your own speed, or you can use it along with guitar lessons. There are no tedious exercises. Instead, there are entertaining pieces of music to play, so learning is fun.

Read a few pages at a time and make sure you understand everything before going on. Do not skip any pages or jump back and forth, or you may miss something important.

Follow each instruction carefully. The guitar is a straightforward in-strument to play as long as you take the time to do everything correctly from the beginning. This way you will avoid getting into bad habits which may limit your playing at a later stage. On the guitar, you will find the right way is not only the best, but also the easiest way in the long run.

This book is the result of many years of playing and teaching the guitar. I hope the benefit of my experience will introduce you to a great deal of pleasure and satisfaction making your own music. Have fun with it.

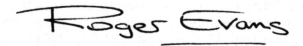

# The Guitar

The guitar is one of the most popular instruments of all time. It makes a very pleasing sound, it is small enough and light enough to carry around and it has a romantic appeal.

The guitar is very versatile. It can be played on its own, or within a group or band. Its tone complements the voice and it gives a good full backing to singing. It has a wide range of notes and makes a good solo and lead instrument. It is a very satisfying and entertaining instrument to play for the beginner, and the expert.

Guitars are made to have either nylon or steel strings. Each type of string has its own distinctive sound and character which suits different kinds of music and different styles of playing.

Nylon strings give a mellow tone and are easier on the fingers than steel strings. The 1st, 2nd and 3rd strings (the thinner strings) are usually a single strand of nylon. The thicker 4th, 5th and 6th strings are nylon strands wound with silver or bronze-plated copper wire.

Steel strings give a brighter, louder sound. Although they are a little harder on the fingers than nylon strings, you soon become used to them. The thinner 1st and 2nd strings are usually plain nickel-plated steel. The thicker 3rd, 4th, 5th and 6th strings are wound with wire.

Nylon-strung and steel-strung guitars may appear similar, but they are made very differently—steel-strung guitars are built more strongly to take the extra stress of steel strings. For this reason, steel strings should never be put on a guitar which was made for nylon strings, or the instrument may be seriously damaged. Nor is it a good idea to put nylon strings on a guitar made for steel strings, because the guitar will sound dead and the strings may buzz. If you have any doubt about which strings are suitable for a particular guitar, ask for advice at your music shop.

Your choice of a nylon or steel-strung guitar should depend on the sound you prefer and the types of music you want to play. In the next few pages are hints to help you choose and buy the guitar which is right for you. If you already have a guitar, read these pages to learn more about your instrument. IF YOU ARE LEFT-HANDED, SEE PAGE 124.

Learn the names of the different parts of the guitar, shown on the facing page, so you will understand what follows.

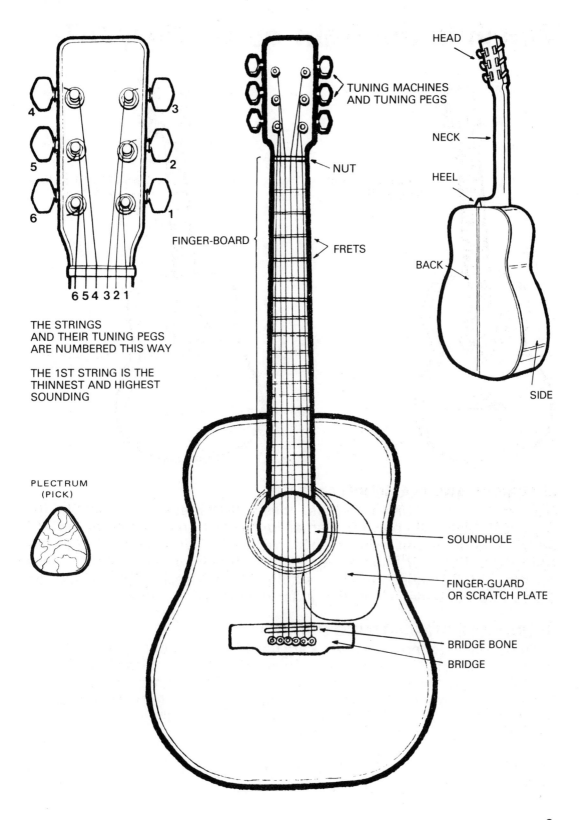

HEAD

TUNING MACHINES
AND TUNING PEGS

NECK

HEEL

NUT

BACK

FINGER-BOARD

FRETS

SIDE

6 5 4 3 2 1

THE STRINGS
AND THEIR TUNING PEGS
ARE NUMBERED THIS WAY

THE 1ST STRING IS THE
THINNEST AND HIGHEST
SOUNDING

PLECTRUM
(PICK)

SOUNDHOLE

FINGER-GUARD
OR SCRATCH PLATE

BRIDGE BONE

BRIDGE

# Which is the right guitar for you?

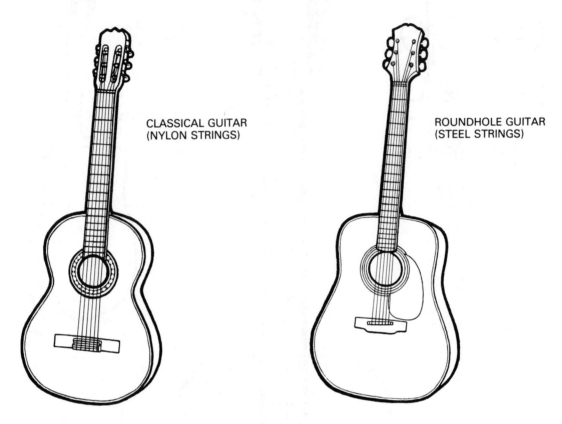

CLASSICAL GUITAR
(NYLON STRINGS)

ROUNDHOLE GUITAR
(STEEL STRINGS)

## CLASSICAL AND FLAMENCO GUITARS

Also known as Spanish Guitars, these instruments are suitable for 'Classical' Style solo playing, Flamenco (Spanish) music and for accompanying singing. The nylon strings are plucked or strummed with the right-hand thumb or fingers—a plectrum should not be used with these guitars. The Flamenco Guitar is similar to the Classical Guitar but has plates to protect the face of the guitar during 'golpe' tapping.

## ROUNDHOLE STEEL-STRUNG GUITARS

These good all-round instruments are used for most popular guitar music —except 'Classical' or Flamenco. They may be fingerpicked, or played 'Pick Style' with a plectrum. They are suitable for accompanying singing, for rhythm, solo and lead playing. Pick-ups may be added to those guitars for playing with an amplifier. The 'Jumbo' is a Roundhole Guitar with an extra large body which gives a deep bass sound.

The 12-String Guitar is similar to a 'Jumbo', but is a more specialised instrument. It is not recommended for absolute beginners.

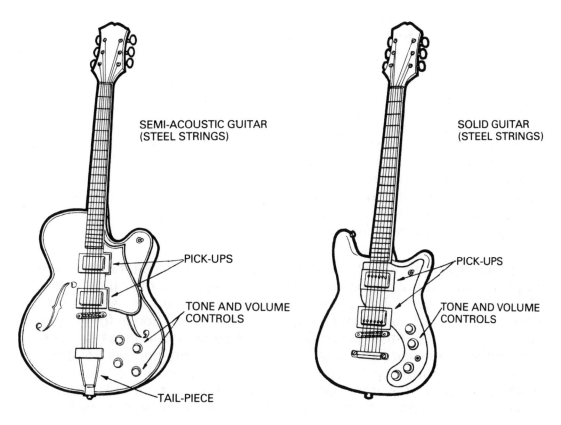

SEMI-ACOUSTIC GUITAR
(STEEL STRINGS)

SOLID GUITAR
(STEEL STRINGS)

PICK-UPS

PICK-UPS

TONE AND VOLUME
CONTROLS

TONE AND VOLUME
CONTROLS

TAIL-PIECE

## SEMI-ACOUSTIC GUITARS

These very slim guitars give enough 'acoustic' (un-amplified) sound for practising, but are otherwise played with an amplifier. They are lighter than Solid Guitars and often have a better tone when amplified.

Cello Guitars are similar but have a thicker body. They are played with or without an amplifier and give a 'chunky' rhythm sound.

## SOLID GUITARS

Solid guitars are only played with an amplifier, as they have no real 'acoustic' sound. They are made in various shapes and styles.

Semi-Acoustic and Solid Guitars have easy 'actions' and are ideal for fast 'electric' playing—Jazz, Rock, Pop, etc. However, they are not recommended for beginners because they are expensive, need an amplifier and have narrow fingerboards which may limit your playing at first.

These guitars are normally played 'Pick Style' with a plectrum.

# How to choose and buy your guitar

Choosing the instrument you play is always an important decision. If you are buying your first guitar, the decision is more difficult because you may not know where to start or what to look for. So, before you do anything, read these friendly words of advice.

First let us dispel the popular, but completely wrong belief that "any guitar will do for learning to play". Your first guitar should be carefully chosen to be fairly easy to play and tune. It should also be versatile enough for you to be able to play different kinds of music on it. For this reason, and to avoid the complications and expense of an amplifier, an 'acoustic' (un-amplified) guitar is recommended. A 'Classical' Guitar, with nylon strings, or a Roundhole Steel-Strung Guitar (see page 10) are particularly good for a first guitar.

If you already have a guitar and want to know if it is suitable for learning to play, check it out as explained in these pages. An old guitar will need checking very carefully indeed. Old instruments can be very good—or very bad. The old guitar which has been around the house for years may well have so many things wrong it could be almost impossible to play, and not worth repairing. If this is the case, or if the guitar is not the right type for the music you want to play, you should look for another instrument. If your guitar seems satisfactory, ask a guitar-playing friend, or your music shop to check it out before trying to play it yourself.

NYLON OR STEEL? Choose the type of guitar which best suits the music you want to play and the sound you want. Do not buy a nylon-strung instrument simply because the strings seem easier on the fingers. If you think you may want to play in a group or band at some time, you will probably do best to choose steel strings, and buy a Roundhole Steel-Strung Guitar. If your leaning is toward 'Classical' or Flamenco music, the choice must be for nylon strings. Guitars of both types are suitable for accompanying singing. If this is the only thing you want to do, choose the guitar with the sound you prefer.

GO WINDOW SHOPPING. Before you decide on anything, go 'window shopping' to see what is available and get an idea of prices. The best places to look are specialist guitar shops or music stores with a good selection of guitars at different prices. Try to find stores where one of the sales staff plays the guitar, so you can be given some expert advice and assistance. Look for guitar and music stores in the 'Yellow Pages' of the telephone directory or in music papers and magazines.

Visit music shops on weekdays, if you can, when they are likely to be able to give you more time. If the store is not busy, ask to be given a demonstration of guitars in the price range you can afford. If you are undecided about steel or nylon-strung guitars, ask to hear one of each. However, do not be pressured into buying before you have visited several stores and compared as many different guitars as possible.

PRICE. Your first guitar need not be expensive, but it should not be the cheapest on the market. Very cheap guitars are normally poor value and will not satisfy you for long. For a little more money you can buy far better guitars which are suitable for learning, and for quite advanced playing.

SECONDHAND GUITARS can be an excellent buy—if you find a good one. However, unless you are an expert, it is unwise to buy a guitar from anyone but a reputable musical instrument dealer. You may find 'bargains' advertised in newspapers, or know someone with a guitar to sell at what appears to be a good price, but these could turn out badly unless you know a lot about guitars. If you are considering a secondhand guitar, take great care to check that everything is right with it and, if possible, get the opinion of an experienced guitarist.

SIZE AND WEIGHT. Avoid heavy acoustic guitars. As a general rule, the more wood there is in an acoustic guitar, the poorer its volume and tone are likely to be. Compare the weight of several guitars of the same type and size, before you decide. (If you are buying a nylon-strung instrument, compare several guitars with nylon strings.) The lightest guitar will usually be the best.

Steel-strung guitars are heavier than nylon-strung guitars, but their method of construction and their louder strings compensate for this. On the whole, smaller bodied steel-strung guitars are a better buy in the lower price ranges. Large guitars, such as 'Jumbos' have to be very carefully designed and very well-made if they are to be any good, and this makes them more expensive. If you want a 'Jumbo', choose very carefully and compare the sound and weight of several.

The weight and size of Solid and Semi-Acoustic guitars depends on the number of pick-ups and type of design. It does not affect the sound, but a very heavy instrument may be tiring to play and a burden to carry around.

Please note, ¾ size guitars are for small children only. They are not recommended for adults, or anyone over the age of ten or eleven years.

HOW LOUD? Compare the volume and tone of acoustic guitars of the same type. If two guitars have a similar tone quality, and are more or less equal in other ways, the louder will normally be the better instrument.

APPEARANCE. Do not choose a guitar simply because it looks good. How it sounds and how it plays is far more important. Fancy decoration does not make a guitar better, but it does make it more expensive. In fact, too much 'plastic' decoration on the face of an acoustic guitar may spoil the tone and reduce the volume.

FINGERBOARD AND NECK. The standard 'Classical' Guitar has a flat fingerboard about 2 inches (50mm) wide at the 'nut'. This is suitable for all normal-sized adult hands. Narrower and slightly curved fingerboards are found on steel-strung guitars. However, for general playing the fingerboard should be at least 1¾ inches (45mm) wide at the 'nut', and flat or only slightly curved. Avoid narrow fingerboards if you have large fingers. Guitars with unduly thick necks are not recommended, particularly if you have small hands.

These general points will help you to choose your guitar. When you come to buy your instrument, see if you can find an experienced guitarist or guitar teacher to go along with you. Unless you already play, ask for the guitar of your choice to be tuned and played for you. If either seems difficult, beware because you could have the same trouble. Here is a short list of other things to check. Take this book along with you to the shop, or make up your own 'Check List'.

BEFORE YOU BUY
1. Check that the fingerboard is straight and the frets all the same height by laying a straight edge over the frets along the fingerboard. Look over the bridge and up along the neck of the guitar to see if it is warped or twisted.

2. Check that the strings are the correct height above the fingerboard. At the 'nut' the strings should be about ¹⁄₁₆" (1.5mm) high, and about ⅛" (3mm) high at the 12th fret. If the strings are too high, the guitar will be hard to play. If they are too low, the strings will buzz on the frets.

3. Play every note by pressing each string behind every fret with a left-hand finger while you pluck the string with your right thumb—each note should sound clearly. Any rattling or buzzing noises when the guitar is played could mean trouble.

4. Look for worn frets on secondhand guitars—particularly the 1st to 5th frets under the 1st, 2nd and 3rd strings. Some wear is normal, but deep

depressions in the frets mean the guitar may be inaccurate, difficult to play and tune, and may buzz unless it is re-fretted.

5. Make sure all six strings are on the guitar. Check each tuning machine by gently turning its peg a little, to see if it adjusts the string to which it is attached. Make sure each string is wound in the right direction on the correct tuning machine. (See drawings on pages 9 and 118.) If any are incorrect, ask for them to be changed around and the guitar re-tuned. If any strings seem old or worn, ask for a new set to be put on, and the guitar put in tune.

6. Examine the face, bridge, sides, head, neck and heel for cracks or splits. On 'Classical' or Roundhole Guitars, there should not be any gaps where the bridge is glued to the face of the guitar. If the guitar is seriously dented or looks as though it may have been dropped or badly repaired, it could be a poor risk.

7. If you are buying an 'electric' guitar, a guitar with a 'pick-up', or an amplifier, also read the advice given on page 113.

If there is anything seriously wrong, do not buy the guitar, at least until it has been corrected or repaired. In most cases, you will be best advised to look for another instrument, even though this may delay your having a guitar. "Buy in haste, regret at leisure" is especially true with musical instruments.

When you buy your guitar, ask for a full written receipt and keep it in a safe place—you may need it for insurance or Customs if you travel.

At the same time, buy a 'Guitar Pitch Pipe' or an 'E Tuning Fork' and a spare set of the correct type of strings.

You should also buy the strongest guitar case you can afford, to protect your instrument. A hard case made of wood, fibreglass or fibreboard is best for expensive guitars, but a soft case or even a thick polythene bag is better than nothing.

If you are a beginner, ask if the guitar is in tune before you leave the shop, and be careful not to knock it on the way home.

There may seem a lot to consider, but if you have followed all the suggestions and checks, you will be sure you have a good guitar which will serve you well and be a joy to play for a long time.

# Taking care of your guitar

Your guitar will last longer and stay in better condition if you take a little time and trouble to look after it.

A guitar can be easily damaged by accident so, when you are not playing it, put it in a safe place, preferably in its case. Always keep it out of the way of clumsy hands and feet, and never leave it on the floor where it could be trodden on, or on a seat where someone may sit on it—many good instruments have been completely destroyed this way! A wardrobe is quite a good place to keep a guitar—lay it flat on top, or stand it up inside one of the corners. If you want to leave it out, use a guitar stand. It is not a good idea to lean a guitar against a wall or anywhere else it could fall over, but if there is no other place, stand it upright in a corner between two inside walls with its face towards the corner.

Wherever you put your guitar, avoid places where there could be a sudden change of temperature or humidity. Never leave it near a radiator, air-conditioning or heating outlet, by a window or in the sun—even in its case. Extreme heat or dryness may cause cracking or splitting, dampness and extreme cold may make the glues soften. In very hot or dry climates and in dry air-conditioning, a 'Guitar Humidifier' should be bought and kept with the guitar inside its case.

If you play outdoors, watch out for dew in the evening and morning. Do not lay the guitar on the ground (it may be trodden on) or on grass as it will be damp. Put it straight back in its case when you have finished playing. When you carry your guitar out of its case, hold it firmly around the neck, near the 'heel'. Treat your guitar as a fragile expensive instrument and you should have no problems.

CLEANING. Gently wipe all parts of the guitar with a soft cloth when you have finished playing. Clean the strings one at a time, by wrapping a corner of a cloth around each of them, and sliding it all the way up and down the string, to remove any dirt or perspiration. This will help the strings to last longer. Modern lacquer finishes are improved by polishing two or three times a year with a guitar polish. However, do not use anything which contains silicones as they leave a permanent coating which cannot be removed if the guitar needs repairing. Keep polish away from the strings and fingerboard and wash your hands before playing.

Before you take your guitar outside of your home, see page 115.
Put on a new set of strings at least every three months, if a string breaks, or if the strings are worn or sound dead. (See page 116.)

# Starting to play

### FINGERS AND FINGERNAILS

On the guitar all sounds are made with the fingers, so it is very important to take good care of your hands.

Cut or file your left-hand fingernails very short, and keep them short and clean. The left-hand fingernails should never be grown past the fingertips because they will get in the way and make it difficult for you to press the strings correctly on to the fingerboard.

File, rather than cut, your right-hand thumbnail and fingernails. They can be level with the fingertips, or grown to about ⅛'' (3mm) above the tips. File the nails of both hands to follow the rounded shape of the fingertips. Keep them smoothly filed—a rough nail makes an unpleasant sound on the strings and is more likely to break. Keep a fine emery board handy in case you break or chip a nail.

Always play with clean hands, but not immediately after washing them as the fingers will be soft after they have been in water. Take special care of your hands, because small cuts or burns can make playing uncomfortable.

At first, the left-hand fingertips may become a little tender, but they can be hardened by dabbing them with a little Surgical Spirit (Rubbing Alcohol) after playing.

### THE FINGERS ARE NUMBERED THIS WAY—

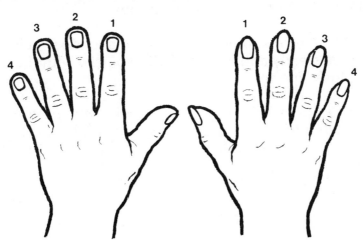

LEFT HAND
Keep nails short and rounded.

RIGHT HAND
Nails may be longer and rounded.

# Holding your guitar

How you hold your guitar and position your hands is very important because it affects how well, and how easily you are able to play. A poor position gives you less control over your fingers and makes playing difficult. So, take the trouble to learn to hold your guitar in a comfortable and relaxed, but correct manner.

Always sit on a steady stool or upright chair—not an armchair, because the arms will get in the way. An easy chair, sofa or bed is not a good place to sit when playing as it is difficult to hold the guitar correctly without a firm upright seat.

Be careful about what you wear when you play. Bulky clothes may restrict you; metal buttons, zippers or jewellery may scratch your guitar.

The 'Classical' position, used by many top players, is considered the best way to hold a guitar. A small footstool or solid box about 6″ (150mm) high is used to raise the left foot. The guitar sits on the left leg and rests against the right thigh for extra support—see facing page.

In the 'Casual' position, the guitar may sit on either thigh. This is not as good as the 'Classical' position, but it is adequate for most playing—as long as the face of the guitar is vertical and the neck is angled slightly upwards.

The guitar should always be held close to the body. The right arm rests on the highest part of the guitar, the right wrist should be relaxed with the fingers hanging at right-angles to the strings.

The left arm and elbow should hang relaxed and loose at your side—the guitar should be steady and completely supported without your left hand touching the instrument.

Lean forward a little while playing and look over the guitar when you want to watch your fingers or see the fingerboard. Keeping the face of the guitar upright at all times is far more important than being able to see your fingers easily. After a little experience, you will begin to find your way around the fingerboard and will not need to look at your fingers as much. (Watch any singer-guitarist and you will find he or she has to play without looking in order to sing out.)

Carefully follow the instructions given here and check your playing position from time to time.

The face of the guitar should be upright.

THE 'CASUAL' POSITION

THE 'CLASSICAL' POSITION

## THE RIGHT HAND

The right hand sounds the strings by plucking or strumming them. The thumb and fingers move in various ways to play one string at a time or several strings together. Steel strings can be played with a plectrum (pick), but this is not recommended while you are starting to play—being able to play with your thumb and fingers is a real advantage, even though you wish to use a plectrum later on.

Start playing with your thumb or thumbnail—later in the book you can learn how to use your fingers or a plectrum if you wish.

Put this book where you can see it and hold your guitar correctly, as explained on the previous page. (Do not touch the guitar with your left hand at this stage.) Position your right hand as shown here, with the thumb resting lightly on the 6th (thickest) string. Your hand should be relaxed, but not floppy. The fingers should be slightly curved and hang at right-angles to the strings, just behind the soundhole.

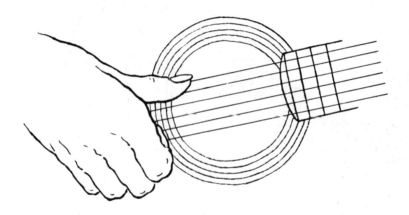

RIGHT HAND POSITION
The wrist is relaxed; the thumb ready to play the 6th string. The fingers are at right-angles to the strings just behind the soundhole.

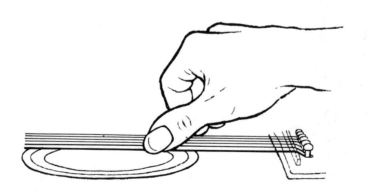

VIEW FROM ABOVE
This is how your right hand should appear to you when you play. The wrist and the rest of the hand is kept away from the strings.

Keep your thumb straight—it should not bend in the middle when you are playing—and keep the rest of the hand away from the strings. Without moving any other part of your hand, push gently downwards with the thumb so it strokes the 6th string and comes to rest on the 5th string. Pluck just hard enough to make a clear-sounding note.

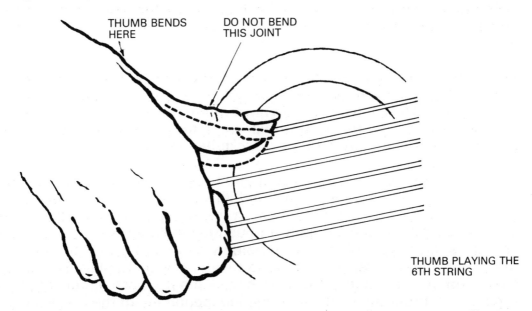

THUMB BENDS HERE

DO NOT BEND THIS JOINT

THUMB PLAYING THE 6TH STRING

Leave the string clear after plucking it—if you touch it, it will stop sounding. Your hand should still be in the same position, so bring your thumb up and around to rest on the 6th string, and pluck down again. Keep trying this until you can play the string smoothly.

## PLAYING WITH A BEAT
Keep your hand in position ready to play, and start counting slowly and evenly: 1—2—3—4—1—2—3—4—1—2—3—4

If you like, tap your foot slowly in time with your counting.

Now, play the 6th string everytime you count '1'. When you can do this without hesitating, play the string everytime you count '1' and '3'. Finally, count very slowly and play it on every beat: 1—2—3—4.

Try playing and counting with each string in turn. Move your hand down and rest the thumb lightly on the 5th string, and play along with your counting. Then the 4th string, and so on.

When you can do this smoothly without hesitating, you will have started to learn something very important—playing in time with the beat.

## THE LEFT HAND

The left-hand fingertips press the strings on to the fingerboard just behind the frets to change the notes on each string. A different note is found at each fret position. The higher up the fingerboard, the higher the notes are on each string. ('High' on the guitar is towards the bridge, 'low' is towards the nut.)

Take special care to position your left hand correctly. The position of the left hand, and the way you hold the guitar, very much affect how easily you can play. The left hand should not support the guitar, it should be free to move around—you can turn over the pages of books or music with your left hand if you are holding your guitar correctly.

Put this book where you can read it and hold your guitar correctly. Then position your left thumb in the middle of the neck, underneath and slightly past the first fret, as shown on the facing page. Your left thumb should be straight—never allow it to bend at the joint. Your wrist should be bent and relaxed, with your left elbow hanging loosely at your side. Arch your fingers over the strings so they are ready to play. The fingers should not bunch together, or be clenched in a fist. Each finger should be separate and relaxed, so it can move independently of the other fingers. The palm of the hand should *never* touch the guitar.

Now, curve your first finger round and lightly press the fingertip on to the 1st (thinnest) string just behind the 1st fret. Press your left thumb gently against the back of the neck and pluck the 1st string with your right thumb. Keep your left hand in position, but relax the thumb. If the note sounded clearly, very good. If not, you are probably not pressing firmly enough, *or* your finger is not close enough to the fret, *or* your finger is right on the fret, *or* your left fingernails are too long. Correct whatever was wrong and keep trying until you get a clear note every time. Relax your hand after each attempt.

Press the strings just hard enough to get a clear note. Too much pressure will tire the fingers and thumb, and slow down your playing.

Take frequent breaks whenever you try anything new and loosen your fingers by flexing them. A good way to relax your fingers is to clench your hand into a tight fist, then throw it away from you so the fingers fly open and outstretched. Do this several times before playing, and whenever you want to loosen your fingers. You do not need to put your guitar down to do this, if you are holding it correctly.

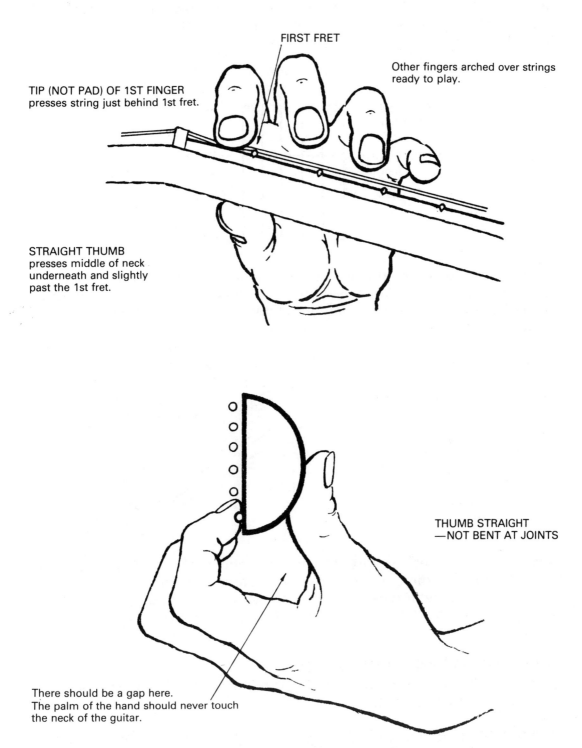

FIRST FRET

Other fingers arched over strings ready to play.

TIP (NOT PAD) OF 1ST FINGER presses string just behind 1st fret.

STRAIGHT THUMB presses middle of neck underneath and slightly past the 1st fret.

THUMB STRAIGHT —NOT BENT AT JOINTS

There should be a gap here. The palm of the hand should never touch the neck of the guitar.

WRIST BENT AND RELAXED

Simple diagrams (called 'Boxes' or 'Windows') show the fingerboard and the position of notes on it. The vertical lines are for the strings, the horizontal lines are for the frets and 'nut'.

STRINGS

(The 1st string is the thinnest string; the 6th string is the thickest string.)

6  5  4  3  2  1

← NUT

← 1ST FRET

← 2ND FRET

← 3RD FRET

A dot on the diagram marks the place where a finger goes to make a particular note. A number beside the dot gives the finger which is to be used to make the note. This diagram shows the note which you played on page 23.

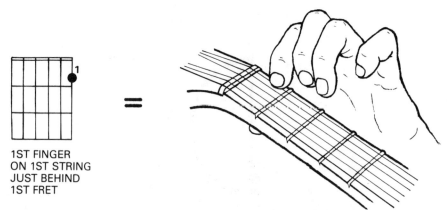

1ST FINGER
ON 1ST STRING
JUST BEHIND
1ST FRET

Always follow these diagrams carefully and make sure you use the correct finger on the correct string, just behind the correct fret. Different notes are made behind each fret on each string, so if your finger is on the wrong string, or behind the wrong fret, you will not be playing the right note.

## OPEN STRINGS AND OPEN NOTES

Some notes are played without a left-hand finger touching a string— these are called 'Open Notes'.

A string which is played without being fingered by a left-hand finger is called an 'Open String'.

Notes are named after letters of the alphabet—
The note on the 1st string open (un-fingered) is called 'e'.
The note on the 1st string just behind the 1st fret is called 'f'.
The note on the 1st string just behind the 3rd fret is called 'g'.

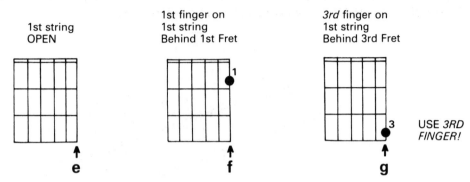

| 1st string OPEN | 1st finger on 1st string Behind 1st Fret | 3rd finger on 1st string Behind 3rd Fret |
| --- | --- | --- |
| e | f | g |

USE *3RD FINGER!*

Hold your guitar in the correct position and find the note 'f'.
(Make sure your left thumb is straight, in the middle of the neck, under-neath and slightly past the 1st fret. Arch your fingers over the strings and press the tip of your first finger onto the 1st string, just behind the 1st fret. The palm should not touch the neck at all.)
Play the note 'f' by plucking the 1st string with your right thumb.

Keep your thumb and the rest of your hand in position, and lift the first finger off the 1st string. Then play the open note 'e'.

Without moving your thumb or the rest of your hand, arch your third finger onto the 1st string, just behind the 3rd fret and play 'g'.

Count the beats slowly and play each note again:

```
    e      f      g      f      e
    1  2  3  4   1  2  3  4   1  2  3  4
```

Count slowly, tap your foot in time with the beat, and play the tune which follows. A thin line is drawn between each set of 4 beats to make them easier to read. Do not slow down at these 'Bar-Lines', but count evenly 12341234 as if they were not there. Play a little more heavily whenever you count '1'. Slowly count the extra beats at the beginning to set your speed. (Note: A 'Double Bar-Line' [ ‖ ] marks the end of the music.)

3 NOTE TUNE

```
|              | g g f e | f f e f | g g f f | e       ‖
|  1  2  3  4  | 1 2 3 4 | 1 2 3 4 | 1 2 3 4 | 1 2 3 4 ‖
```

## A DIFFERENT FINGER FOR EACH FRET

At the '1st position', the 1st finger is used to press *any* of the strings behind the 1st fret, the 2nd finger is used to press *any* of the strings behind the 2nd fret, the 3rd finger is used to press *any* of the strings behind the 3rd fret and the 4th finger is used to press any of the strings behind the 4th fret, when single notes are played.

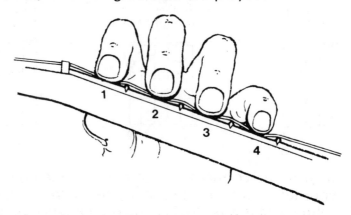

At this stage you should not slide any finger up or down a string to play different notes.

## TRAINING YOUR FINGERS

Practise this for a few minutes everytime you play to help train your fingers to use the correct frets and move independently of one another.

Lightly press your fingers on the 6th string as shown above—4th finger behind the 4th fret, 3rd finger behind the 3rd fret, and so on. (If this is too much of a stretch at first, start with your 1st finger behind the 5th fret instead, with each of the other fingers one fret higher.)

Press your thumb against the back of the neck, press down with the 4th finger and pluck the 6th string, to play the note at the 4th fret.
Then, lift off the 4th finger and play the note at the 3rd fret.
Next, lift off the 3rd finger and play the note at the 2nd fret.
Finally, lift off the 2nd finger and play the note at the 1st fret.

Take a break, then play the notes in the opposite order—1st fret, 2nd fret, 3rd fret and then the 4th fret note.

Also try playing the same pattern of notes on the other strings in turn— the 6th string, then the 5th string, then the 4th string, and so on.

Practise this very little at a time. Relax your hand frequently by resting the palm on a table with your thumb and fingers outstretched.

# How to tune your guitar

Tuning is the most important thing you have to learn. Even simple music sounds good when your guitar is in tune, but if the guitar is out of tune everything played on it will sound unpleasant. Be patient when you first tune your guitar—it will become easier after a while.

Find somewhere quiet where you will not be overheard or distracted when you tune your guitar. You will need either a 'Guitar Pitch Pipe', an 'E' Tuning Fork or another instrument to give you the note for the first (thinnest) string. After that the guitar can be tuned to itself.

**WHERE TO FIND THE NOTE FOR THE 1ST STRING**

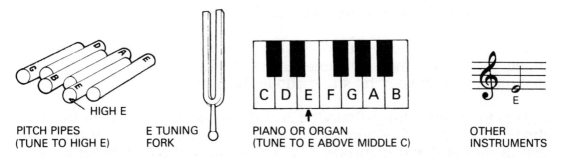

PITCH PIPES
(TUNE TO HIGH E)

E TUNING
FORK

PIANO OR ORGAN
(TUNE TO E ABOVE MIDDLE C)

OTHER
INSTRUMENTS

PITCH PIPES and 'E' TUNING FORKS are sold fairly inexpensively in music stores, and are handy to keep in a guitar case. Pitch pipes have a pipe for tuning each string, however it is best to use just one pipe. Find the highest sounding of the two 'E' pipes, hold it in your mouth and blow it gently and evenly to give the note for the first string. An 'E' Tuning Fork gives the most accurate note. Hold the handle between your right thumb and first finger and strike the prongs against your knee. Then hold the end of the handle on the bridge of the guitar with the prongs in the air, and you should hear the note you need.

A PIANO or ORGAN will also give the note you need. Use the note 'E' just above 'Middle C' in the middle of the keyboard. An organ gives a perfect note if you turn off the 'Vibrato' and other effects. (If you tune to a piano, your guitar may not be in tune with other instruments, because pianos are not all tuned to the same 'pitch'. This does not matter if you play on your own, or with that piano.) You can also get your note 'E' from other instruments—or another guitar, as long as the other guitar is in tune.

The note 'E' on a Pitch Pipe, Tuning Fork or other instrument will not sound exactly the same as your 1st string, because each has a different tone. Match the sounds as closely as possible when you are tuning.

Each string is tuned by gently turning its tuning peg, a little at a time. Turning it one way tightens the string and makes it sound higher. Turning the other way slackens the string and makes it sound lower. Hold each tuning peg between your left thumb and 1st finger and make sure you turn the correct peg for each string—see facing page.

1. Tuning the 1st string. Blow your 'High E' pitch pipe evenly, or play the note 'E' on the tuning fork or other instrument. While the note sounds, pluck the 1st string. (Pluck with a left-hand finger if you use a tuning fork.) If the 1st string sounds higher than the note 'E', slacken it by turning its tuning peg a little. If the string sounds lower, tighten it a little. (A ¼ turn at a time is best.) If you are not sure whether it is higher or lower, leave it as it is and listen again—first play the note and then the string. If you are still not sure, slacken the string a little. If the string sounds *more* out of tune, you are going the wrong way and should tighten it instead.

Continue to adjust your 1st string a little at a time, until it sounds neither higher nor lower than the note 'E' on the pitch pipe, tuning fork or instrument. Then your 1st string should be in tune.

2. Tuning the 2nd string. Press the 2nd string just behind the 5th fret with the tip of left-hand 2nd finger, *and keep it there*. Play the 1st string twice, wait a moment and then play the 2nd string. If the 2nd string sounds higher, turn its tuning peg a little to slacken it. If it sounds lower, tighten it a little and compare the strings again. (Play the 1st string first.) Continue tuning the 2nd string (with your finger behind the 5th fret) until it sounds the same as the 1st string open.

3. Press the 3rd string behind the FOURTH fret with your 2nd finger. Play the 2nd string twice, then play the 3rd string. Keep fingering the 3rd string at the 4th fret, and tune it a little at a time, until it sounds the same as the 2nd string open.

4. Press the 4th string behind the FIFTH fret, and gently tune it until it sounds the same as the 3rd string open.

5. Press the 5th string behind the 5th fret, and gently tune it until it sounds the same as the 4th string open.

6. Press the 6th string behind the 5th fret, and gently tune it until it sounds the same as the 5th string open.

Your guitar should now be in tune.

# TUNING YOUR GUITAR

1

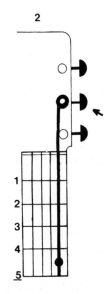

TURN ARROWED PEG TO
TUNE 1ST STRING TO
'HIGH E' PITCH PIPE,
'E' TUNING FORK OR
'E' ABOVE 'MIDDLE C'

## TURN ARROWED PEG
## TO TUNE EACH STRING

2

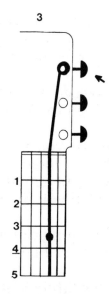

PRESS 2ND STRING
BEHIND 5TH FRET
AND TUNE TO
1ST STRING OPEN

3

PRESS 3RD STRING
BEHIND **FOURTH** FRET
AND TUNE TO
2ND STRING OPEN

4

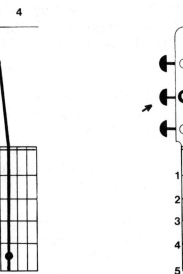

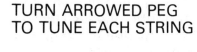

PRESS 4TH STRING
BEHIND 5TH FRET
AND TUNE TO
3RD STRING OPEN

5

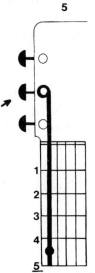

PRESS 5TH STRING
BEHIND 5TH FRET
AND TUNE TO
4TH STRING OPEN

6

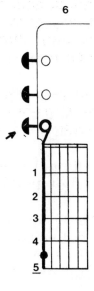

PRESS 6TH STRING
BEHIND 5TH FRET
AND TUNE TO
5TH STRING OPEN

# Tuning Hints

1. Check your tuning every time you play. Tune your guitar in another room before you play for anyone else. Before playing your guitar with another instrument, tune it to the other instrument (see page 27).

2. Take your time tuning and make sure each string is in tune before going on to the next.

3. When you are tuning one string to another, listen first to the string which is already in tune, and play it twice to fix the sound in your mind. Then, wait a moment before playing the string which is to be tuned. This will help you to hear the difference between the two strings.

4. Do not pluck the strings too hard or the sound will be distorted. However, pluck hard enough to hear each string clearly.

5. If the string you are tuning seems to be getting more and more out of tune, you are going the wrong way. Turn the tuning peg the other way and see if the string gets closer to being in tune. If in doubt, always slacken rather than tighten strings to avoid straining them or the guitar. When the strings sound nearly the same, turn the tuning pegs very little.

6. If two strings sound very close, and you are not sure if they are in tune, play them *quickly* one after the other. If you hear a sour, wavering beat, or feel a wavering vibration in the guitar, the strings are not perfectly in tune with each other.

7. Make sure your first finger is always just behind the correct fret and press each string straight on to the fingerboard. If the string is 'bent' the note will be altered and you will not be able to get in tune.

8. Be careful not to knock the tuning pegs when carrying the guitar or taking it out of its case, as this could put it out of tune.

If you have real difficulty tuning your guitar, wait a while and try again. If this does not work, ask for the help of someone who plays any musical instrument—they should be able to tell if you are tuning correctly—or take your guitar to your music shop and ask them to help.

If you happen to break a string, see page 116.
If you think there may be something wrong with your guitar see page 123.

# More notes—and tunes to play

The next notes—**b**, **c**, and **d**—are on the 2nd string. They are shown here with the 1st string notes which you have already played.

Try playing each note one after the other—**b c d c b**
(Be sure to use your 3rd finger behind the 3rd fret for the note '**d**'.)

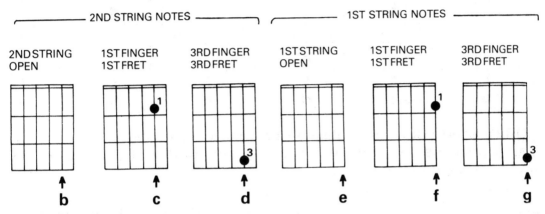

Now play the notes on the 1st and 2nd strings, counting the beats and tapping your foot in time—

| COUNT | c | | d | | e | | f | | g | | f | | e | | d | | c | | |
|---|---|---|---|---|---|---|---|---|---|---|---|---|---|---|---|---|---|---|---|
| | 1 | 2 | 3 | 4 | 1 | 2 | 3 | 4 | 1 | 2 | 3 | 4 | 1 | 2 | 3 | 4 | 1 | 2 | 3 | 4 |

Always keep your fingers on each note until the next finger is ready to play—'Walking' your fingers from one note to the next makes your playing smooth and professional sounding. It also helps train your fingers to move in the correct way.

Some notes last longer than others in the tune which follows. This is no problem if you count slowly and evenly, and play each note in time with the beat which is shown for it. (Do not stop counting or slow down at the 'Bar-Lines'.) Slowly count the extra beats at the beginning to set your speed.

## ODE TO JOY by Beethoven

| COUNT | | | e ——— f | g | g f e d | c c d e | e ——— d d | |
|---|---|---|---|---|---|---|---|
| | 1 2 3 4 | 1 2 3 4 | 1 2 3 4 | 1 2 3 4 | 1 2 3 4 | | |

| | e ——— f | g | g f e d | c c d e | d ——— c c | |
|---|---|---|---|---|---|---|
| | 1 2 3 4 | 1 2 3 4 | 1 2 3 4 | 1 2 3 4 | | |

The three tunes which follow are played with the notes you have learned. The note diagrams are repeated, so you can refer to them without turning the page. Remember to play each note with the correct finger.

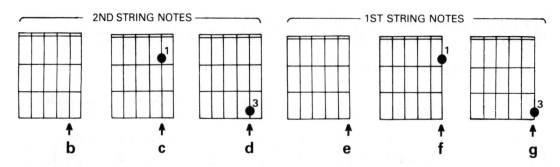

2ND STRING NOTES          1ST STRING NOTES

b    c    d    e    f    g

**BOBBY SHAFTOE**—an English and American folk song.
You can see here how the words of the song fit the tune. Tap your foot and slowly count the beat.

|   |   |   |   | Bob-by | Shaf-toe's | gone to | sea — | Sil - ver | buck-les |   |
|---|---|---|---|---|---|---|---|---|---|---|
|   |   |   |   | c c c f | e g e c | d d d |   |   |   |   |
| COUNT | 1 2 3 4 | 1 2 3 4 | 1 2 3 4 | 1 2 3 4 |

| on his knee — | he'll come back and | mar -ry me — | bon -ny Bob -by | Shaf —— toe. |
|---|---|---|---|---|
| b d b — | c c c f | e g e c | d f d b | c — c — |
| 1 2 3 4 | 1 2 3 4 | 1 2 3 4 | 1 2 3 4 | 1 2 3 4 |

**SKIP TO MY LOU**—an American folk song.

|   |   |   |   | Lost my part-ner | what'll I do — | lost my part-ner |
|---|---|---|---|---|---|---|
|   |   |   |   | e e c c | e e g — | d d b b |
| COUNT : | 1 2 3 4 | 1 2 3 4 | 1 2 3 4 | 1 2 3 4 |

| what'll I do — | Lost my part-ner | what'll I do ____ | Skip to my Lou,my | dar — ling. |
|---|---|---|---|---|
| d d f — | e e c c | e e g — | d d e d | c — c — |
| 1 2 3 4 | 1 2 3 4 | 1 2 3 4 | 1 2 3 4 | 1 2 3 4 |

Practise these tunes until you can play them smoothly in time with the beat.

Before you start to play any tune, take a few moments to think about it. Sing or hum the first few notes to yourself so you get the right feeling for the tune and start counting and playing at the correct speed.

Take time to learn this next step properly.

1. Put your 1st finger on the 2nd string behind the 1st fret to make the note '**c**'. Check that the 1st finger is not touching the 3rd or 1st strings at all, then play the 3rd, 2nd and 1st strings one after the other. Three clear notes should sound. If any note sounds dead or buzzes, your finger is not in the right place, or your fingernails are too long. Relax, correct what was wrong, and try again. (See drawing 1.)

2. Hold the note '**c**', then flatten your 1st finger so it presses the 2nd string *and* the 1st string, both behind the 1st fret. (Drawing 2.) Now play the 2nd and 1st strings. Keep trying until you hear two clear notes. Then keep your 1st finger in place and go on to step 3.

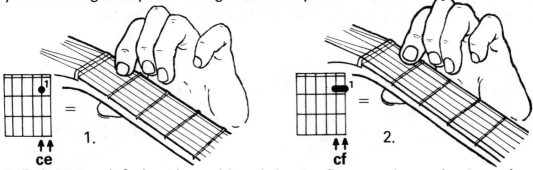

3. Relax your left thumb, and bend the 1st finger to leave the 1st string open again (as in drawing 1). Play the 3rd, 2nd and 1st strings so you get three clear-sounding notes again.

Repeat these three steps, stroking your right thumb smoothly across the 1st and 2nd strings, so both notes sound together—

| e | e | f | f | e |
|---|---|---|---|---|
| c | c | c | c | c |
| 1 | 2 | 3 | 4 | 1   2   3   4 |

Make sure you can do this evenly in time with the counting, then play the next tune which has these notes at the end.

## GO AND TELL AUNT RHODY—American Folk Song.

| | | | | Go | and | tell | Aunt | Rho — | dy ——— | ,Go | and | tell | Aunt |
|---|---|---|---|---|---|---|---|---|---|---|---|---|---|
| | | | | **e** | **e** | **e** | **d** | **c** | **– c –** | **d** | **d** | **d** | **f** |
| COUNT : | 1 | 2 | 3 | 4 | 1 | 2 | 3 | 4 | 1   2   3   4 | 1 | 2 | 3 | 4 |

| Rho — | dy —, | Go | and | tell | Aunt | Rho — | dy | her | old | grey goose is | dead, f | e | |
|---|---|---|---|---|---|---|---|---|---|---|---|---|---|
| **e** | **d** | **c** | **–** | **g** | **g** | **g** | **f** | **e** | **– e** | **e** | **d** | **d** | **e d** | **c** | **c** | **c** | **–** |
| 1 | 2 | 3 | 4 | 1 | 2 | 3 | 4 | 1 | 2 | 3 | 4 | 1 | 2 | 3 | 4 | 1 | 2 | 3 | 4 |

33

# Starting to Play Chords

A chord is made when two or more notes are played together. The notes played together on two strings (page 33) were simple chords, but most chords are made by playing at least four strings at the same time.

Chords are named after their most important notes. There are 'C Chords', 'D Chords', and so on. They are shown in diagrams like single notes.

The 'C Chord' is made like this:

1. Put your 1st finger on the 2nd string, behind the 1st fret.
2. Add your 2nd finger on the 4th string, behind the 2nd fret.
3. Add your 3rd finger on the 5th string, behind the 3rd fret.

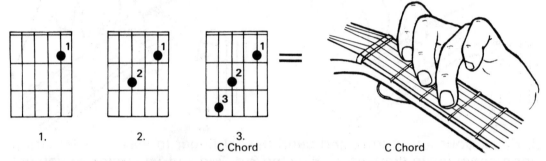

1.  2.  3. C Chord   C Chord

When your fingers are in place, press the back of the neck with your left thumb, and play the C Chord by brushing your right thumb across the strings with a smooth, quick downward stroke.

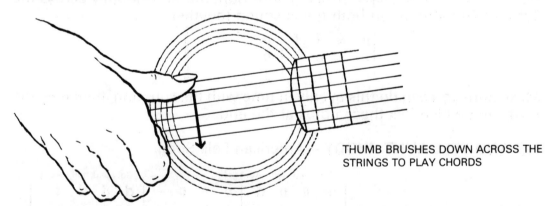

THUMB BRUSHES DOWN ACROSS THE STRINGS TO PLAY CHORDS

The right thumb should quickly *stroke* the strings, without digging in, so they sound at the same time. The whole hand can move with the thumb; the wrist and forearm turns, but does not go up and down. The C Chord sounds best if the 6th string is not played, so try to start your thumb stroke with the 5th string.

When you play chords, touch only the strings you need and make sure your fingers are close behind the correct frets—or some of the strings may sound dead or buzz. Check the fingering of chords by playing each string one after the other to make sure every note sounds clearly.

If a chord sounds unpleasant when all the strings are played together, your fingers are in the wrong places, or the guitar is out of tune.

The next chord is called 'G7' (G SEVEN). It is similar to the C Chord, but the fingers are all on different strings. G7 is made like this:

1. Put your 1st finger on the 1st string, behind the 1st fret.
2. Add your 2nd finger on the 5th string, behind the 2nd fret.
3. Add your 3rd finger on the 6th string, behind the 3rd fret.

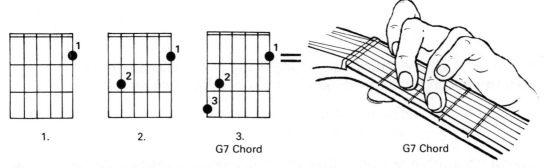

1.  2.  3.
G7 Chord    G7 Chord

When your fingers are in place, press the back of the neck with your left thumb, and play the G7 Chord.

C Chords and G7 Chords are normally found together, so you need to practise changing from one to the other—

1. Put your fingers lightly in place for the C Chord.

2. Hold the C Chord and work out where your fingers have to go for 'G7'. (The fingers stay in the same shape, but the 1st finger moves to the 1st string, and the 2nd and 3rd fingers go to the 5th and 6th strings.)

3. Now, move your fingers smoothly to make the G7 Chord. Play the chord, then relax your hand with your fingers still in place.

4. Work out where the fingers go for the C Chord. (Each finger moves over one string.) Move your fingers to the C Chord, and play it.

When changing chords and playing single notes, keep your fingers close to the strings so they do not have to move further than necessary.

Next, change chords in time with a beat. Count *very* slowly at first, and move your fingers to the other chord when you count "and" (&).

|   |   | C |   | G$_7$ |   | C |   | G$_7$ |   | C |
|---|---|---|---|---|---|---|---|---|---|---|
|   |   |   | CHANGE |   | CHANGE |   | CHANGE |   | CHANGE |   |
| 2 | & | 1 | & | 2 | & | 1 | & | 2 | & | 1 |

Now, count slowly and tap your foot—1 2 3 4 1 2 3 4, and so on. Without breaking the beat, fit "and" (&) between each "4" and "1". (Do not tap or slow down on "&" as this falls between the beats.)

1    2    3    4 & 1    2    3    4 & 1    2    3    4

Next, play each chord four times, changing to the other chord on "&".

| C | / | / | / | G$_7$ | / | / | / | C | / | / | / | etc. |
|---|---|---|---|---|---|---|---|---|---|---|---|---|
| 1 | 2 | 3 | 4 & 1 | 2 | 3 | 4 & 1 | 2 | 3 | 4 & 1 | 2 | 3 | 4 & |

A stroke (/) after a chord name means the chord is to be repeated. Play the chord once for its name, and once for *each* stroke:

C / = PLAY C CHORD TWICE          G$_7$ / / = PLAY G$_7$ CHORD 3 TIMES

C / / / = PLAY C CHORD 4 TIMES

Speed up gradually when you can change chords without pausing. Make sure you change chords in the right places and play each chord the correct number of times. Keep the right-hand rhythm and foot-tapping going if your miss a chord change—and any mistakes will not be noticed.

Chords give a 'backing' harmony and rhythm to a tune. However, they do not normally give the melody, which is usually sung or played by another instrument. When you play 'Chord Backings', sing or hum the melody or try to hear it in your head. Before you start, play the first few notes, or even the whole tune to fix the melody in your head.

**BOBBY SHAFTOE.** Play the first few notes (c c c f e g e) to fix the tune in your mind, then sing or hum with the chord backing.

|   |   |   |   | Bob-by Shaf-toe's | gone to sea | – | Sil - ver buck-les |
|---|---|---|---|---|---|---|---|
|   |   |   |   | C / / / | C / / / | G$_7$ / / / |   |
| COUNT AND TAP | 1 2 3 4 | 1 2 3 4 | 1 2 3 4 & 1 | 2 3 4 |

| on his knee – | He'll come back and mar - ry me – | Bon - ny Bob - by | Shaf —— toe — |
|---|---|---|---|
| G$_7$ / / / | C / / / | C / / / | G$_7$ / / / | C / / / |
| 1 2 3 4 & 1 | 2 3 4 | 1 2 3 4 & 1 | 2 3 4 & 1 | 2 3 4 |

# How to practise

If you can, practise every day for at least 20 minutes. Regular daily practice is far better than trying to play for several hours once or twice a week. The more often you play, the better you will become.

Practise in a quiet place where you will not be overheard. Nothing is worse than having someone listen while you are learning to play.

Be patient. Make sure you can play each piece smoothly at the right speed before going on to the next tune. However, try to learn something new every week, even if it is a simple tune or a couple of chords.

Start playing everything slowly. When you can play correctly and evenly, gradually work up to the proper speed. If you try to play quickly too soon, you will never play well.

Relax while you are playing. Give your fingers a rest now and then, and stop playing if they become tired or stiff.

Do not be discouraged if your playing does not seem to be improving very quickly. As long as you practise regularly and keep learning, your playing will gradually become better all the time. If anything seems awkward, practise it a little every day and it will soon become easier.

Plan your practice to make the best of your time, like this:

1. Flex your fingers to loosen them. Warm your hands if they are cold.

2. Check your tuning, and re-tune your guitar if necessary.

3. For a few minutes, practise using all your left-hand fingers to play the notes at different frets (page 26). This will strengthen your hand and make the 4th (little) finger ready for playing when you need it.

4. Practise something new, or something which you do not play well. If a few notes or chord changes slow you down in a tune, practise them separately until you can play them without hesitating.

5. Finally play music you already know. Even when you are playing for fun, polish your playing by correcting any mistakes or bad habits.

# Starting to read music

Learning to read music is easier than most people think. There is no real mystery to it—a piece of music is a set of instructions which tells you how to play (or sing) a particular tune or song. Different signs tell you everything about the music—which notes to play, when and how to play them and how long they should sound.

Already you know more than you may realise about reading music. You know the names of some notes which you can play, and have learned to fit them in with beats which you count. The rest is not difficult. Soon you will play more notes and learn to recognise them in a piece of music.

Of course, you could learn to play the guitar without reading music. You could get by if you have the flair for picking everything up very quickly by copying other players, or if you restrict yourself to basic backings for tunes you know well. However, you will be able to learn new songs and tunes more easily, quickly and correctly and understand more about the music you want to play, if you take a little time to learn to read music. Most guitarists find it is a real advantage to be able to read music; many of those who do not read regret they did not learn when they started to play the guitar. Now is the best time for you to learn and take the next step towards becoming a good guitarist.

**HOW NOTES ARE NAMED**

As you know, notes are named after letters of the alphabet, and each note sounds higher than the note before—'d' sounds higher than 'c', 'e' is higher than 'd', and so on. Only seven letters are used for note names—from 'a' to 'g'. After 'g', the next note higher is another 'a'—

a  b  c  d  e  f  g  a  b  c  d, and so on.

Notes are given the same names because they sound very much alike, in spite of being higher or lower than each other. Play 'g' on the 1st string behind the 3rd fret and compare it with the 3rd string open, which is also called 'g'. These notes are very similar even though the note on the 3rd string sounds lower.

(In this part of the book, note names are shown with small 'lower case' letters, so they will not be confused with chord names by beginners.)

## HOW NOTES ARE WRITTEN

Notes are written on a 'Stave' which has five lines. Each note has its place on one of the lines *or* in one of the spaces—one note is on the line, the next note higher is in the space above, and so on. (Important. The lines *do not* refer to the strings of the guitar.)

At the beginning of each line of music which can be played on the guitar there is a sign— 𝄞 —called a 'Treble Clef' or 'G Clef'. This clef marks the position of the note 'g' on the second line up.

G CLEF

POSITION OF NOTE 'g'
ON 2ND LINE

As long as you can remember the position of 'g', you can work out all the other notes from it—

'g' is on the second line, 'a' is in the space above, 'b' is on the middle line, and so on. Going downwards, 'f' is in the space under 'g', and 'e' is on the bottom line.

HIGH NOTES AT TOP OF STAVE

LOW NOTES AT BOTTOM OF STAVE

This is how these notes appear in music—

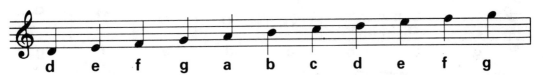

d    e    f    g    a    b    c    d    e    f    g

The 'stems' of notes can go up (♩) or down (♩), it does not make any difference to the notes.

Work out the names of the notes in the music which follows and write them underneath each note in pencil. Then play the tune. (You have already played these notes on the 1st and 2nd strings—see page 31).

As you know from the tunes you have been playing, some notes last for more beats than other notes. In music, the shape of a note tells us how many beats it should last.

♩ is a Quarter Note. In most music it lasts for 1 beat.

♩ is a Half Note. In most music it lasts for 2 beats.

𝅝 is a Whole Note. In most music it lasts for 4 beats.

You can count the beats and fit in the notes with your counting—exactly as you have done with the tunes you have been playing.

EACH QUARTER NOTE LASTS THIS LONG     EACH HALF NOTE LASTS THIS LONG     EACH WHOLE NOTE LASTS THIS LONG

## SOME NOTES ON THE 1ST, 2ND AND 3RD STRINGS

Play these notes one after the other—you already know most of them.

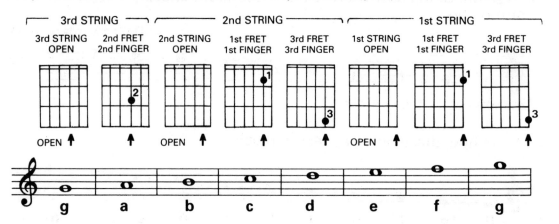

Try playing this little tune. (Remember you should not stop or slow down at the 'Bar-Lines'.)

**SUR LE PONT D'AVIGNON**—A French folk song.
Play this tune to practise reading music. You can also practise playing the chords—the chord names are shown over the music.

Notice that the second line of the music is almost the same as the first line —only the end is different. Always look for parts of music which are repeated, it will save you having to work it out more than once.

# Are you playing correctly?

Check your playing regularly to avoid getting into bad habits:

Are you holding your guitar correctly? See page 19.
Is your right hand in the correct position? See pages 20 and 21.
Is your left thumb in the correct position? Are you keeping it straight when you play? See page 23.
Do you keep your left-hand fingers curved and close to the strings when you are playing? See page 23.
Are you using the correct finger for notes behind each fret? See page 26.
Are you playing evenly, without quickening up or slowing down?
Are you keeping your guitar in tune, and checking it before playing?
Do you remember to clean the strings after playing? See page 16.
Are you keeping your guitar in a safe place? See page 16.

If there is anything you did not understand in the book, read it again.

# More chords to play—F, Am, Dm, E7

Some tunes can be played with two chords, but most music needs at least three. The next chord is found in many different tunes.

### THE F CHORD

Two strings are pressed at the same time by the 1st finger for this chord —exactly like the '**f**' and '**c**' notes you played together earlier.

Make the F Chord like this:

1. Put your 1st finger on the 1st and 2nd strings behind the 1st fret. (The pad of the finger should be flat on the strings.)

2. Arch your 2nd finger on to the 3rd string behind the 2nd fret. Take care it does not touch the 2nd string at all.

3. Add your 3rd finger on the 4th string behind the 3rd fret.

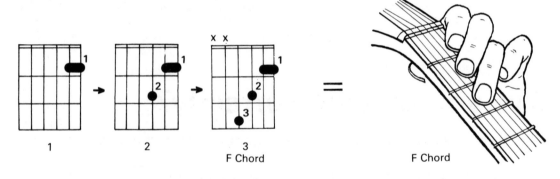

When your fingers are in place, press the back of the neck with your left thumb and play the F Chord, starting with the 4th string.

The 'x' signs over the 5th and 6th strings mean these strings should not be played with the F Chord.

Practise the F Chord a little everytime you play. At first you may not always make a clear sound on all strings, but keep trying, and before long you should be able to play it.

This chord is important because it is a step towards more advanced guitar playing.

The F Chord and C Chord are often found together in many tunes. Practise changing from one to the other like this:

1. Put your fingers in place for a C Chord, and play it.

2. Relax your left thumb and fingers, but keep them in place.

3. Twist your hand slightly, so the pad of your 1st finger presses the 1st and 2nd strings, and move the 2nd and 3rd fingers to the 3rd and 4th strings. Then play the F Chord.

To return to the C Chord, relax and twist your hand the other way, and at the same time move your 2nd and 3rd fingers over one string each.

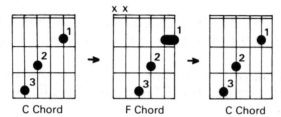

C Chord      F Chord      C Chord

The chords you have learned so far are called 'Major Chords' and there is another completely different set of chords called 'Minor Chords'. Minor Chords are made with slightly different notes but have a very different feeling about them. Minor Chords sometimes seem sad, but they can also be exciting or merry, depending on how they are used in music. Often you will find them mixed with Major Chords to add interest to the backing of a tune.

Major Chords are usually known by the note name only—'C Major' is usually written 'C'. Minor Chords are marked with a small 'm' after the note name—'A Minor' is often written 'Am'.

Try playing the following Minor Chords, and the E7 Chord which is often found with them. These chords should be fairly easy for you now, as long as you use the correct fingering. The 6th string should not be played with the D Minor Chord, because it will not sound correct.

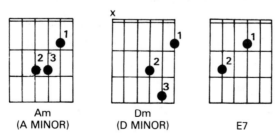

Am      Dm      E7
(A MINOR)    (D MINOR)

43

# Changing Chords

Before going any further, play all the chords you have learned so far—

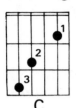  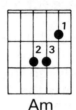  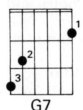 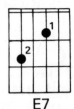

| C | F | G7 | Am | Dm | E7 |

Try to move all of your fingers at the same time, and change chords in one smooth movement. Relax your thumb between different chords.

Lightly hold each chord before changing to the next and check to see if any of the fingers stay in the same place, or same shape—

C and G7 are the same shape, but the fingers are on different strings. E7 and A Minor are similar, but E7 uses one less finger—and the fingers all move over one string.
Leave your 1st finger on the 1st string, when changing from F or D Minor to G7, and so on.

Change chords slowly at first, counting evenly. Keep your foot tapping and your right hand playing a steady beat, without slowing down.

When you can play the following 'Chord Sequences' smoothly, you will know how to make the chord changes for hundreds of tunes—

| C / F / | C / $G_7$ / | C / F / | $G_7$ / C / ‖
  1   2   3   4     1   2   3   4     1   2   3   4     1   2   3   4

Minor Chords mixed with Major Chords:—

| C / Am / | Dm / $G_7$ / | C / Dm / | $G_7$ / C / ‖
  1   2   3   4     1   2   3   4     1   2   3   4     1   2   3   4

Minor Chords have a different feeling here:—

| Am / Dm / | $E_7$ / / / | Am / Dm / | $E_7$ / Am / ‖
  1   2   3   4     1   2   3   4     1   2   3   4     1   2   3   4

Now all six chords together —

| C / $E_7$ / | Am / F / | Dm / $G_7$ / | C / / / ‖
  1   2   3   4     1   2   3   4     1   2   3   4     1   2   3   4

# More about music

At the beginning of all music there are two numbers, or a sign— $\mathbb{C}$ .
This is the 'Time Signature' and it tells us how many beats should be
counted for each 'Bar'. (A 'Bar' is the space between two 'Bar-Lines'.)

If the top number is '3', there should be 3 beats—

IS COUNTED: | 1    2    3 | 1    2    3 | AND SO ON

Try playing chords while you count 3 beats to the Bar. Make the first beat
stronger than the other 2 beats in each Bar—

| C / / | C / / | G₇ / / | C / / ‖
| 1   2   3 | 1   2   3 | 1   2   3 | 1   2   3 |

The tunes you have played so far in this book have had 4 beats.
This music would have '$\mathbb{C}$' (for Common Time) or $\frac{4}{4}$ at the beginning—

OR ... IS COUNTED | 1 2 3 4 | 1 2 3 4 |

## DOTTED NOTES
A small dot after a note means it should last half as long again—

| 1    2    3 | 1    2    3 |

HALF NOTE
LASTS 2 BEATS

DOTTED HALF NOTE
LASTS 3 BEATS

## TIED NOTES
Notes are often made longer by joining them to the next note with a
curved line called a 'Tie'. The first note then lasts for the total number of
beats of the notes 'tied' together—

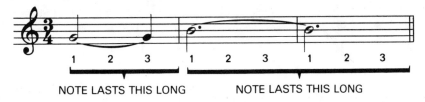

| 1    2    3 | 1    2    3 | 1    2    3 |

NOTE LASTS THIS LONG          NOTE LASTS THIS LONG

This only applies if the next note has the same name and position.

All these musical signs are found in the tunes on the next two pages.

# SOME NOTES ON THE 4TH, 5TH AND 6TH STRINGS

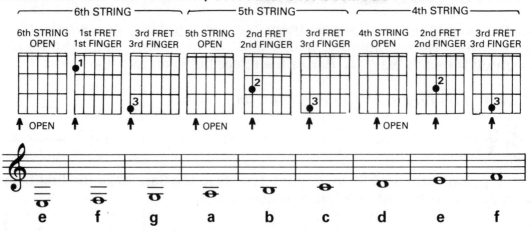

The 4th string notes take us to the bottom of the Stave, so the 5th and 6th string notes are written on short lines called 'Leger Lines' which provide extra lines and spaces under the Stave. Notes on Leger Lines can be worked out in the same way as other notes—'d' is in the space under the Stave, so 'c' is on the first Leger Line below, 'b' is in the space under the first Leger Line, and so on. Look up these notes in the diagram at the top of this page, until you know them.

Play the notes on the 4th, 5th and 6th strings, saying the name of each note as you play it. Then play the next tune. When you know it, hum it to yourself while you play the chords. It has 3 beats to the Bar.

**TUM BALALAIKA**—a Yiddish folk song.

## NOTES YOU SHOULD KNOW BY NOW

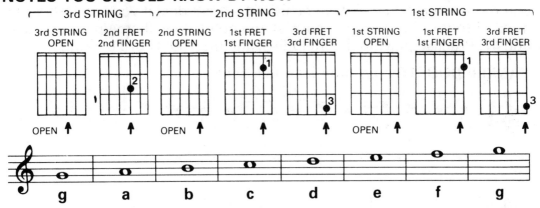

Play the tunes on this page and the next to practise reading music and playing chords. The words to the songs are shown so you can sing along with the chord backings if you wish. Look up any notes you do not remember in the diagrams at the top of these two pages.

## DOWN IN THE VALLEY—an American folk song.

Look through these tunes before you play them and see how many notes you remember. You will have achieved a great deal if you can remember most of them. If you are not sure of any notes, look them up on pages 46 and 47. Practise playing the melodies, and then the chord backings.

## YANKEE DOODLE—an American folk song.

Yan-kee Doo-dle went to town, a— rid-ing on a po — ny, He
stuck a feather in his cap and called it mac— a— ro—— ni——.

## EARLY ONE MORNING—an English folk song.

Ear—— ly one mor——ning, just as the sun was ris—— ing, I
heard a maid- en sing-ing in the val————ley be—low.

Oh, don't de——ceive—— me— Oh—— nev-er leave— me—

How— can you use— a— poor— maiden so.

48

# Should you play with a Plectrum?

Whether or not you need to learn to play with a plectrum (or 'Pick' as it is also known) depends on the music you want to play, and the type of guitar you have. A plectrum is normally only used on guitars with steel strings for certain styles of playing. A plectrum does not suit the nylon-strung guitar or the music normally played on it, and it may damage the strings.

Lead and Rhythm Guitar styles (electric and acoustic) are normally played with a plectrum. So, if you play a steel-strung guitar and want to join a group or band at some stage, you should learn to use one.

Folk, Blues and Country music is often played with a plectrum, but you also need to play 'fingerstyle' for these types of music. 'Pick Style' guitar music can usually be played either way. The best advice, if you have a steel-strung guitar, is to learn to play both ways—with a plectrum, *and* with your right-hand thumb and fingers.

If you decide to play some of your music with a plectrum, choose one which is medium size and medium weight, not too flexible, or too rigid. 'Plectra' (*not plectrums!*) are usually made of tortoise-shell or plastic. Your music shop should be able to offer a selection. They are not expensive, so try one or two different types, and buy a spare.

Hold the plectrum fairly firmly between the right thumb and 1st finger, as shown below. Play single notes in the same way as you played with your thumb—pick straight down on a string, just hard enough to get a clear note, and let the plectrum come to rest on the next string. When you play chords, let the plectrum glide over the strings, without digging in. Aim to get clear smooth-sounding chords, without clicking noises, and be careful not to scratch the face of the guitar.

Try playing the tunes and chords you have learned with a plectrum.

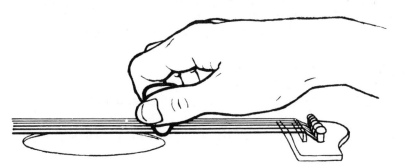

Hold your plectrum like this between the thumb and 1st finger.

Play just behind the Soundhole.

# Become your own Bass Player

Straight chord backings like those you have been playing are fine for many tunes, and are not just for beginners. These backings sound good in a group or band which has a bass player, but if you play on your own they may become a little boring if used for every tune. You can make your own music more varied and interesting by becoming your own bass player, like this—

Put your fingers in place for a C Chord.
1. Hold the C Chord and pluck the 5th string, letting your thumb or plectrum come to rest on the 4th string.
2. Play the rest of the chord by brushing your thumb or plectrum smoothly and quickly over the 4th, 3rd, 2nd and 1st strings.

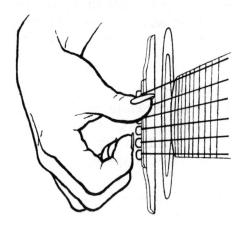

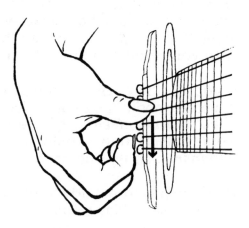

1. Thumb plucks bass string and comes to rest on the next string.

2. Thumb plays chord by brushing smoothly over the remaining strings.

Now try it with other chords—

Put your fingers in place for the F Chord.
1. Hold the chord and pluck the 4th string. (Your thumb or plectrum should come to rest on the 3rd string this time.)
2. Play the rest of the chord, starting your stroke on the 3rd string.

Put your fingers in place for the G7 Chord.
1. Hold the chord and pluck the 6th string.
2. Play the rest of the chord, starting your stroke on the 5th string.

Finally go back to the C Chord, pluck the 5th string and then play the rest of the chord.

What you have just played can be shown quite simply, like this—

(The number tells you which string is to be plucked, the arrow means the thumb or plectrum is to play the rest of the strings.)

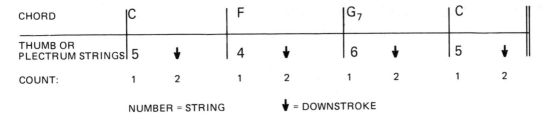

| CHORD | C | | F | | G$_7$ | | C | |
|---|---|---|---|---|---|---|---|---|
| THUMB OR PLECTRUM STRINGS | 5 | ↓ | 4 | ↓ | 6 | ↓ | 5 | ↓ |
| COUNT: | 1 | 2 | 1 | 2 | 1 | 2 | 1 | 2 |

NUMBER = STRING    ↓ = DOWNSTROKE

Always finger the chord *before* you play the Bass Note.

You have been playing a two beat rhythm. The three beat rhythm has a single Bass Note followed by *two* downstrokes played by the thumb or plectrum. Try it. Count slowly and tap your foot in time with the beat.

| $\frac{3}{4}$ | C | | | F | | | G$_7$ | | | C | | |
|---|---|---|---|---|---|---|---|---|---|---|---|---|
| | 5 | ↓ | ↓ | 4 | ↓ | ↓ | 6 | ↓ | ↓ | 5 | ↓ | ↓ |
| | 1 | 2 | 3 | 1 | 2 | 3 | 1 | 2 | 3 | 1 | 2 | 3 |

The most important Bass Note for a chord is the note which has the same name as the chord—Here you played a C Bass Note with the C Chord, an F Bass Note with the F Chord and a G Bass Note with the G7 Chord.

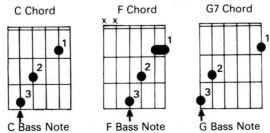

C Chord        F Chord        G7 Chord

C Bass Note    F Bass Note    G Bass Note

If another Bass Note is needed before changing to the next chord, a different note can be chosen from within the chord. Try this—

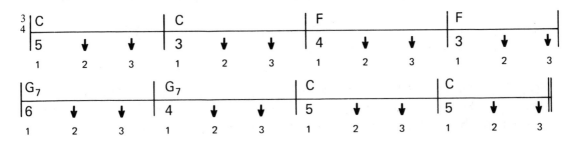

| $\frac{3}{4}$ | C | | | C | | | F | | | F | | |
|---|---|---|---|---|---|---|---|---|---|---|---|---|
| | 5 | ↓ | ↓ | 3 | ↓ | ↓ | 4 | ↓ | ↓ | 3 | ↓ | ↓ |
| | 1 | 2 | 3 | 1 | 2 | 3 | 1 | 2 | 3 | 1 | 2 | 3 |
| | G$_7$ | | | G$_7$ | | | C | | | C | | |
| | 6 | ↓ | ↓ | 4 | ↓ | ↓ | 5 | ↓ | ↓ | 5 | ↓ | ↓ |
| | 1 | 2 | 3 | 1 | 2 | 3 | 1 | 2 | 3 | 1 | 2 | 3 |

51

'Down in the Valley' becomes more interesting if played with Bass Notes. Go back to page 47 and play the melody to fix it in your mind. Then, play the Bass Note and Chord Backing shown here. Sing or say the words to the song in time with your playing.( $\frac{3}{4}$ means 3 beats to the Bar.)

## DOWN IN THE VALLEY—Bass Notes with Chords.

| $\frac{3}{4}$ | G₇ | | | C | | | C | | | C | | |
|---|---|---|---|---|---|---|---|---|---|---|---|---|
| | 6 | ↓ | ↓ | 5 | ↓ | ↓ | 3 | ↓ | ↓ | 5 | ↓ | ↓ |
| | 1 | 2 | 3 | 1 | 2 | 3 | 1 | 2 | 3 | 1 | 2 | 3 |
| | Down | in | the | val___ | | | ley___ | | | ___ | | , the |

| C | | | G₇ | | | G₇ | | | G₇ | | |
|---|---|---|---|---|---|---|---|---|---|---|---|
| 3 | ↓ | ↓ | 6 | ↓ | ↓ | 4 | ↓ | ↓ | 6 | ↓ | ↓ |
| val __ley | so | | low___ | | | | | | | | |

| G₇ | | | G₇ | | | G₇ | | | G₇ | | |
|---|---|---|---|---|---|---|---|---|---|---|---|
| 4 | ↓ | ↓ | 6 | ↓ | ↓ | 4 | ↓ | ↓ | 6 | ↓ | ↓ |
| Hang | your | head | o___ | | | ver. | | | | | |

| G₇ | | | C | | | F | | | C | | |
|---|---|---|---|---|---|---|---|---|---|---|---|
| 4 | ↓ | ↓ | 5 | ↓ | ↓ | 4 | ↓ | ↓ | 5 | ↓ | ↓ |
| Hear | the | wind | blow.___ | | | | | | | | |

FOUR BEAT RHYTHMS ( $\frac{4}{4}$ ) usually go Bass Note—Chord—Bass Note—Chord: (Count 1 2 3 4 1 2 3 4, and so on.)

| $\frac{4}{4}$ | C | | | | F | | | | G₇ | | | | C | | | |
|---|---|---|---|---|---|---|---|---|---|---|---|---|---|---|---|---|
| | 5 | ↓ | 3 | ↓ | 4 | ↓ | 3 | ↓ | 6 | ↓ | 4 | ↓ | 5 | ↓ | 3 | ↓ |
| | 1 | 2 | 3 | 4 | 1 | 2 | 3 | 4 | 1 | 2 | 3 | 4 | 1 | 2 | 3 | 4 |

Play A Minor and D Minor Chords with the Bass Notes shown here:

| $\frac{4}{4}$ | C | | | | Am | | | | Dm | | | | G₇ | | | | C | | | |
|---|---|---|---|---|---|---|---|---|---|---|---|---|---|---|---|---|---|---|---|---|
| | 5 | ↓ | 3 | ↓ | 5 | ↓ | 6 | ↓ | 4 | ↓ | 5 | ↓ | 6 | ↓ | 4 | ↓ | 5 | ↓ | 3 | ↓ |
| | 1 | 2 | 3 | 4 | 1 | 2 | 3 | 4 | 1 | 2 | 3 | 4 | 1 | 2 | 3 | 4 | 1 | 2 | 3 | 4 |

Some four beat rhythms have one Bass Note followed by three chords:

| $\frac{4}{4}$ | C | | | | Am | | | | Dm | | | | G₇ | | | | C | | | |
|---|---|---|---|---|---|---|---|---|---|---|---|---|---|---|---|---|---|---|---|---|
| | 5 | ↓ | ↓ | ↓ | 5 | ↓ | ↓ | ↓ | 4 | ↓ | ↓ | ↓ | 6 | ↓ | ↓ | ↓ | 5 | ↓ | ↓ | ↓ |
| | 1 | 2 | 3 | 4 | 1 | 2 | 3 | 4 | 1 | 2 | 3 | 4 | 1 | 2 | 3 | 4 | 1 | 2 | 3 | 4 |

Play Bass Note and Chord backings to tunes in this book, and any other tunes you know. Always take care to use the right rhythm for each tune—if the tune has 3 beats, play the 3 beat rhythm, and so on.

Playing with the thumb is fine for slow tunes, but there is another better way to play Bass Note and Chord backings—with your 1st finger and thumb. Bass Notes are still plucked by the thumb, but chords are played with the nail of the 1st finger. This 'technique' can be used in many different ways to make your playing more versatile and interesting. It is also faster and more accurate than using the thumb on its own. If you play a steel-strung guitar, you can get almost the same effect with a plectrum, but you should also learn to play with your thumb and fingers as this is an important step towards learning Fingerpicking.

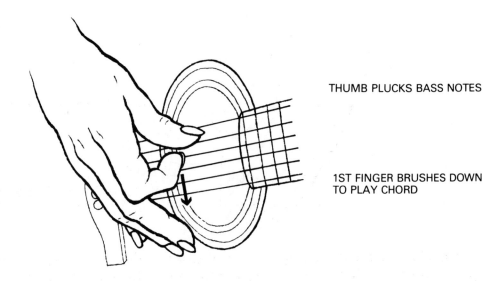

THUMB PLUCKS BASS NOTES

1ST FINGER BRUSHES DOWN TO PLAY CHORD

Finger a C Chord and play the 'Brush Stroke' like this—

1. Pluck the 5th string with your thumb.
2. Play the rest of the chord by brushing your 1st finger quickly down across the 4th, 3rd, 2nd and 1st strings.
3. Pluck the 3rd string with your thumb.
4. Play the rest of the chord with your 1st finger.

The top of the hand should not move when the 1st finger and thumb play the strings. Now play this: (↓ = 1st FINGER DOWNSTROKE)

| 4/4 | C | | F | | G7 | | C | |
|---|---|---|---|---|---|---|---|---|
| 1st FINGER | ↓ | ↓ | ↓ | ↓ | ↓ | ↓ | ↓ | |
| THUMB STRING | 5 | 3 | 4 | 3 | 6 | 4 | 5 | |
| | 1 2 3 4 | | 1 2 3 4 | | 1 2 3 4 | | 1 2 | |

Try the 'Brush Stroke' with tunes you have learned.

The downward Brush Stroke played by the 1st finger works very well as a backing for many tunes. However, if you play in a group or with a number of singers, you may want the backing to be stronger. If this is the case, play the chord strokes with all of the fingers held together, instead of using the 1st finger on its own.

## DOWN-UP BRUSH STROKES
A different effect is made by playing downward and then upward Brush Strokes after each Bass Note. The 1st finger brushes down, as before, and then plays the same strings again on its way back up.

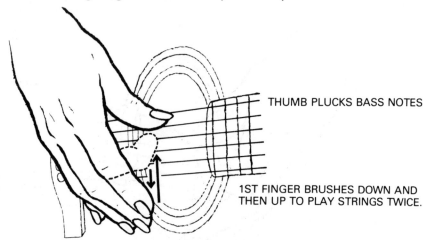

THUMB PLUCKS BASS NOTES

1ST FINGER BRUSHES DOWN AND THEN UP TO PLAY STRINGS TWICE.

Before playing these examples, count out the timing to get the rhythm right. Count slowly at first and tap your foot in time with the beat. (Your foot should not tap on '&' because this falls between the beats.)

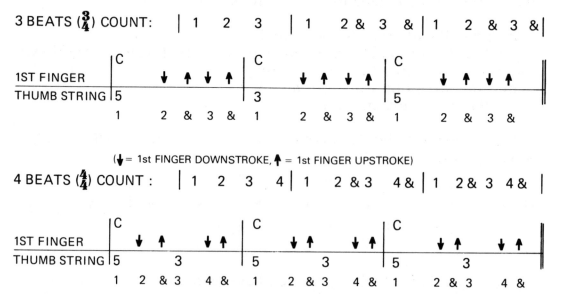

## BEAUTIFUL, BEAUTIFUL BROWN EYES—an American folk song.

This tune can be played with down-up Brush Strokes or just down strokes. Play the melody first, so you know how it goes, then play the backing. Look up any notes you may not remember on pages 46 and 47.

# How to play melodies with chords

Brush Stroke patterns can be adapted to play some melodies backed by their chords. It does not work for every tune, but when performed well, this style of playing sounds almost like two guitars being played together.

In the next tune, the Bass Notes are replaced by melody notes. Pluck the strings shown and you will be playing the melody. Play the chord strokes a little softer than normal, so the melody stands out from the backing. Remember to put your fingers in place for each chord before plucking the string which is marked. (If you play with a plectrum, try playing this tune both ways—play the melody and chords with your plectrum, then play the same thing with your thumb and 1st finger.)

**JOHNNY TODD**—an English sailor's song.

Briskly

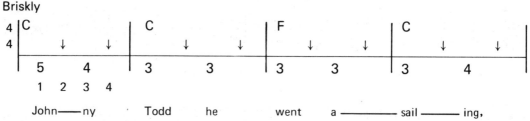

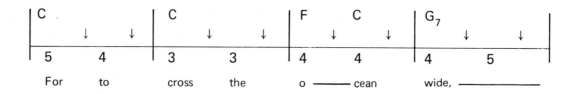

56

'Johnny Todd' is a simple tune to play with Brush Strokes because all the melody notes are within the chords. There are other tunes like it, but most tunes need some melody notes which are not in the chords. These other melody notes can often be played by taking a finger off a chord, or by putting a finger on a different string—or by changing the Brush Stroke pattern slightly to fit in more notes.

Try this different Brush Stroke pattern. There is only one Brush Stroke in each Bar, but there are three melody or bass notes:

|  | C | F | $G_7$ | C |
|---|---|---|---|---|
| 1st FINGER | ↓ | ↓ | ↓ | ↓ |
| THUMB | 5    4  3 | 4    3  4 | 6    5  4 | 5 |
| COUNT | 1  2  3  4 | 1  2  3  4 | 1  2  3  4 | 1  2 |

Now try this 'run' which leads from the C Chord to the F Chord.
The 2nd finger is taken off the C Chord for one note, then put back for the next note. (Move your finger at the 'dotted lines'.)

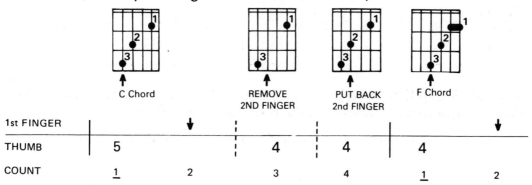

C Chord     REMOVE 2ND FINGER     PUT BACK 2nd FINGER     F Chord

| 1st FINGER |  | ↓ |  |  |  | ↓ |
|---|---|---|---|---|---|---|
| THUMB | 5 |  | 4 | 4 | 4 |  |
| COUNT | 1 | 2 | 3 | 4 | 1 | 2 |

This style of playing can be written in a simple system used by many guitarists and guitar teachers—

String numbers are given as usual for notes which are in the chords. Notes which are to be changed are shown by a small number next to the string number. This gives the fret at which the note is to be played—

$4^0$ = 4th string open     $4^2$ = 4th string at the 2nd fret, and so on.

The run you have just played would be written like this—

|  | C |  |  | F |  |
|---|---|---|---|---|---|
| 1st FINGER |  | ↓ |  |  | ↓ |
| THUMB | 5 |  | $4^0$  $4^2$ | 4 |  |
|  | 1 | 2 | 3  4 | 1 | 2 |

The 2nd finger is lifted off or replaced to play notes in the runs on this page and the tune on the next page, like this—

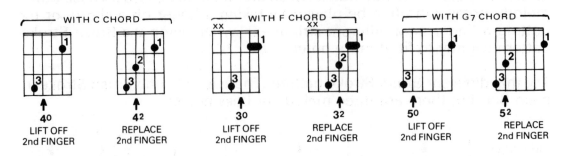

| WITH C CHORD | | WITH F CHORD | | WITH G7 CHORD | |
|---|---|---|---|---|---|
| 40 | 42 | 30 | 32 | 50 | 52 |
| LIFT OFF 2nd FINGER | REPLACE 2nd FINGER | LIFT OFF 2nd FINGER | REPLACE 2nd FINGER | LIFT OFF 2nd FINGER | REPLACE 2nd FINGER |

Here are some bass note runs which are often played together. You have already played the first run—from the C Chord to the F Chord. The other run is from the G7 Chord back to the C Chord. These runs often lead from one chord to the next in Brush Stroke backings and melody playing.

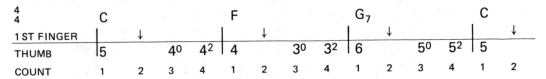

$\frac{4}{4}$

| | C | | | | F | | | | G7 | | | | C | | |
|---|---|---|---|---|---|---|---|---|---|---|---|---|---|---|---|
| 1ST FINGER | | ↓ | | | | ↓ | | | | ↓ | | | | ↓ | | |
| THUMB | 5 | | $4^0$ | $4^2$ | 4 | | $3^0$ | $3^2$ | 6 | | $5^0$ | $5^2$ | 5 | | | |
| COUNT | 1 | 2 | 3 | 4 | 1 | 2 | 3 | 4 | 1 | 2 | 3 | 4 | 1 | 2 | | |

Another Brush Stroke pattern is good for backings and melody playing. Count it out loud to learn the rhythm before playing it—

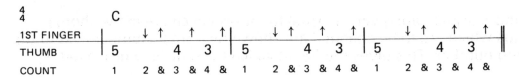

| 1 | 2 & 3 & 4 & | THUMB | DOWN-UP | THUMB-UP | THUMB-UP |
|---|---|---|---|---|---|

The Brush Stroke should play the 3rd, 2nd and 1st strings only. (Reminder. ↓ = 1st finger downstroke, ↑ = 1st finger upstroke.)

$\frac{4}{4}$

| | C | | | | | | | | | | | | | | |
|---|---|---|---|---|---|---|---|---|---|---|---|---|---|---|---|
| 1ST FINGER | | ↓ | ↑ | ↑ | ↑ | | ↓ | ↑ | ↑ | ↑ | | ↓ | ↑ | ↑ | ↑ |
| THUMB | 5 | | 4 | | 3 | 5 | | 4 | | 3 | 5 | | 4 | | 3 |
| COUNT | 1 | 2 | & | 3 | & 4 & | 1 | 2 | & | 3 | & 4 & | 1 | 2 | & | 3 | & 4 & |

Practise this pattern for a few minutes each day. When you can play it evenly, try playing it with the bass runs—

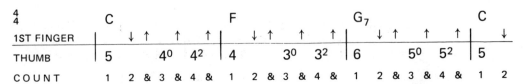

$\frac{4}{4}$

| | C | | | | F | | | | G7 | | | | C | | |
|---|---|---|---|---|---|---|---|---|---|---|---|---|---|---|---|
| 1ST FINGER | | ↓ | ↑ | ↑ | ↑ | | ↓ | ↑ | ↑ | ↑ | | ↓ | ↑ | ↑ | ↑ | ↓ |
| THUMB | 5 | | $4^0$ | $4^2$ | 4 | | $3^0$ | $3^2$ | 6 | | $5^0$ | $5^2$ | 5 | | | |
| COUNT | 1 | 2 & 3 & 4 & | 1 | 2 & 3 & 4 & | 1 | 2 & 3 & 4 & | 1 2 | | | | | | | | |

The next tune can be played with either of the Brush Stroke patterns shown on the facing page. If you want to play the simpler pattern at first, ignore all the upstrokes (marked ↑), but come back and learn to play the more advanced version later on.

Notice that the 1st and 3rd lines of this tune are the same. The Brush pattern changes in the 3rd Bar of every line to give variety. (This pattern was explained at the bottom of page 54.)

In this tune, the chord names are shown only where a chord is to change —the C Chord is played for the first two Bars, the F Chord is played for the next two Bars, and so on. This is the way chords are shown in most music.

**IT'S HARD, YES IT'S HARD**—an American folk song.

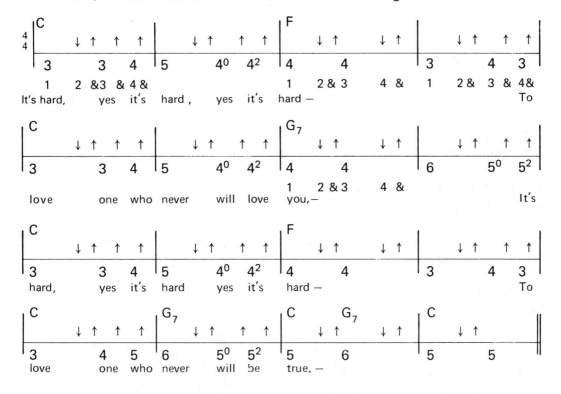

Notes which do not have words under them are 'fillers' and runs which link the separate phrases of the melody, so the effect is continuous. If the song were being sung, this is where the singer would take a breath and the backing would 'fill-in'. Play these notes a little softer.

# More Chords—G, B7, Em and D

Now is the time to start practising chords which use the 4th (little) finger, so you will be able to play them when you need them. Practise these chords a little each day and you will soon find them no more difficult than other chords.

The G Chord is similar to G7, but has the 4th finger on the 1st string just behind the 3rd fret. Play the G7 Chord, add your 4th finger on the 1st string, take off your 1st finger and play the G Chord. Try this a few times, then relax your hand.

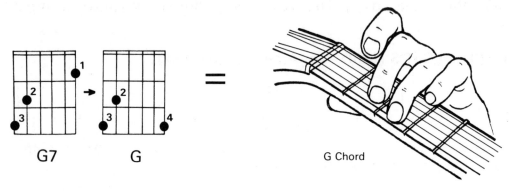

G7      G         =      G Chord

When you can do this, try going straight to the G Chord. Put your 2nd and 3rd fingers in place, then add the 4th finger.

Try changing from the C Chord to the G Chord and back again—the 2nd and 3rd fingers stay in the same shape, but move over one string each.

Some people play the G chord without using the 4th finger, but this is not recommended if you wish to progress beyond basic playing.

'B7' is another chord played with the 4th finger. Put your fingers in place like this—

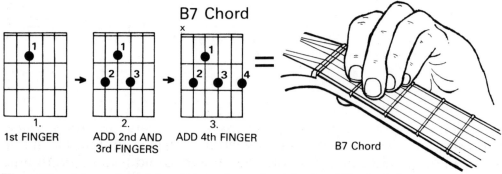

B7 Chord

1.
1st FINGER

2.
ADD 2nd AND
3rd FINGERS

3.
ADD 4th FINGER

=

B7 Chord

The 6th string should not be played with the B7 chord.

Here are two other chords to practise. Be sure to use the correct fingering for each chord, because it will affect your playing in the future.

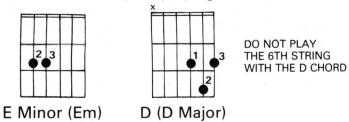

DO NOT PLAY
THE 6TH STRING
WITH THE D CHORD

E Minor (Em)          D (D Major)

Always make sure you play the right chords. You should never play a Minor Chord instead of a Major Chord with the same letter name. D Minor is not the same as the D (D Major) Chord. Play them both and hear the difference. Play these Chord Sequences to practise changing chords—

| G / Em / | Am / D / | G / C / | D / G / ‖

| Em / D / | C / $B_7$ / | Em / Am / | $B_7$ / Em / ‖

# Rhythm Guitar Playing

This style of playing provides the backing chords and rhythm for other instruments and singing in groups and bands. It is also suitable for the singer-guitarist who wants strong chord backings for some songs.

If you managed to play all of the Brush Stroke patterns, the rhythms shown here should be easy. Practise them, then play them to tunes and chord sequences which you have learned. No bass notes are needed, just play the chord strokes with your thumb or plectrum. Use $\frac{4}{4}$ patterns for tunes with 4 beats, and $\frac{3}{4}$ patterns for tunes with 3 beats. Count out loud and play each pattern again and again to feel the different rhythms.

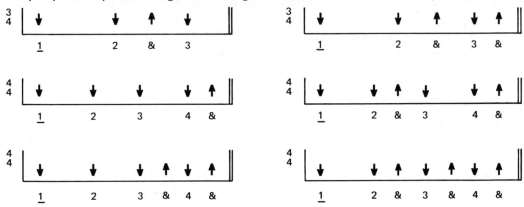

# How to start Fingerpicking

Fingerpicking is a popular and versatile style of playing. It gives attractive backings and pleasant melodic guitar solos. Fingerpicking may seem very expert and complicated when you watch someone playing it, but it is just a few steps from Brush Stroke playing—if you learn a little at a time and practise every pattern until you can play it smoothly and correctly.

In fingerpicking, the thumb plays a regular pattern of bass or melody notes (as it did with Brush Strokes), while the fingers pluck (pick) other strings to give backing or melody notes. The thumb plucks down and the fingers pluck upwards.

A good right-hand position is essential. Your hand should be relaxed, but not loose.

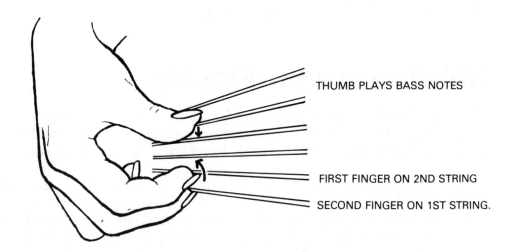

THUMB PLAYS BASS NOTES

FIRST FINGER ON 2ND STRING

SECOND FINGER ON 1ST STRING.

Rest your thumb on the 5th string ready to play the Bass Note.
Place the tip of your FIRST finger on the 2nd string.
Place the tip of your SECOND finger on the 1st string.
Your fingers should be curved and relaxed. Make sure each finger is on the correct string. (The SECOND finger should be on the 1st string!)

Keep your right hand in place and finger a C Chord with your left hand.
1. Pluck the 5th string with your thumb.
2. Clench both fingers slightly, so the 1st and 2nd strings are plucked together. After playing, the fingers should lift clear of the strings, then move down, ready to pluck again. The fingers should stay as close to the strings as possible without actually touching them.

Play the pattern a few times, and then try it with the thumb playing alternate bass notes—first the 5th string, then the 3rd string:

| | C | | | | | | | |
|---|---|---|---|---|---|---|---|---|
| 4/4 | | | | | | | | |
| 2ND FINGER STRING | | 1 | | 1 | | 1 | | 1 |
| 1ST FINGER STRING | | 2 | | 2 | | 2 | | 2 |
| THUMB STRINGS | 5 | | 3 | | 5 | | 3 | |
| COUNT: | 1 | 2 | 3 | 4 | 1 | 2 | 3 | 4 |

This pattern can be used for some backings instead of Brush Strokes.

In the next pattern, each finger plucks separately. Put your thumb and fingers in place before you start. (Put your thumb on the 5th string, the 1st finger on the 2nd string, and the 2nd finger on the 1st string.)
Finger a C Chord with your left hand.

1. Pluck the 5th string with the thumb.
2. Pluck the 2nd string with your 1st finger.
3. Pluck the 1st string with your 2nd finger.

| | C | | | | | | G7 | | | C | |
|---|---|---|---|---|---|---|---|---|---|---|---|
| 3/4 | | | | | | | | | | | |
| 2ND FINGER STRING | | | 1 | | | 1 | | | 1 | | |
| 1ST FINGER STRING | | 2 | | | 2 | | | 2 | | | |
| THUMB STRINGS | 5 | | | 5 | | | 6 | | | 5 | |
| COUNT: | 1 | 2 | 3 | 1 | 2 | 3 | 1 | 2 | 3 | 1 | |

Change to the G7 Chord and a different bass note in the third Bar.

Now, a similar pattern, with an extra note played by the 1st finger.
Put your thumb and fingers in place as before, and finger a C Chord.

1. Pluck the 5th string with your thumb.
& Pluck the 2nd string with your 1st finger.
2. Pluck the 1st string with your 2nd finger.
& Pluck the 2nd string again with your 1st finger.

Continue playing and counting until you can play smoothly. Then try a full 4 beat backing pattern with alternate Bass Notes—

| | C | | | | | | | | | | | | | | | | |
|---|---|---|---|---|---|---|---|---|---|---|---|---|---|---|---|---|---|
| 4/4 | | | | | | | | | | | | | | | | |
| 2ND FINGER STRING | | | 1 | | | | 1 | | | | 1 | | | | 1 | | |
| 1ST FINGER STRING | | 2 | | 2 | | 2 | | 2 | | 2 | | 2 | | 2 | | 2 |
| THUMB STRINGS | 5 | | | | 3 | | | | 5 | | | | 3 | | | | |
| COUNT: | 1 | & | 2 | & | 3 | & | 4 | & | 1 | & | 2 | & | 3 | & | 4 | & |

IMPORTANT! The top of the hand should not move at all when the thumb and fingers pluck the strings. (Some players rest the little finger on the Bridge or Face of the guitar to steady the hand, but this is NOT a good idea as it tightens the hand and may cause cramping.)

A slightly different pattern is perfect for many tunes with 3 beats. This pattern is similar to the previous one, but the 1st finger plucks only once after the second Bass Note in each Bar.

Put your fingers and thumb in position as before, and finger a C Chord with your left hand. Slowly count 1 & 2 & 3 & before starting—

| 3/4 | C | | | | | | | | | |
|---|---|---|---|---|---|---|---|---|---|---|
| 2ND FINGER STRING | 1 | | | 1 | | | 1 | | | |
| 1ST FINGER STRING | 2 | 2 | 2 | 2 | 2 | 2 | 2 | 2 | 2 | |
| THUMB STRINGS | 5 | | 3 | 5 | | 3 | 5 | | 3 | |
| COUNT | 1 & | 2 & | 3 & | 1 & | 2 & | 3 & | 1 & | 2 & | 3 & | |

When you can play the pattern smoothly, practise it thoroughly with the chord sequences which follow. This pattern is important because it fits many songs and is needed for several tunes in this book.

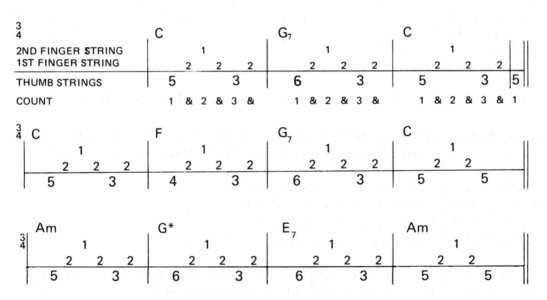

* See page 60 if you do not remember this chord.

The patterns you have learned so far are suitable for backing singing with the bass notes and chords shown here. Some of the patterns can also be used for melody playing, if the bass notes are replaced with melody notes played by the thumb.

The next tune has all of the melody notes in the chords, and can be played with the 3 beat pattern shown on the facing page. It introduces a new chord—the E Chord—which is the same shape as 'A Minor', but with each finger moved over one string. Be careful not to confuse the E Chord with E7 or E Minor—they are all different.

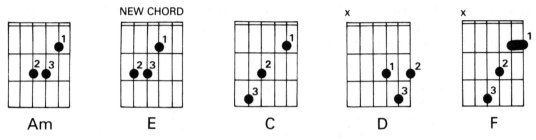

## HOUSE OF THE RISING SUN—Melody Playing.

Play the chord backing to the tune to practise the chord changes. Then try fingerpicking it. Put your right thumb and fingers in place and count the beat slowly 1 & 2 & 3 & , before you start. Pluck the strings shown, and you will be playing the melody with your thumb.

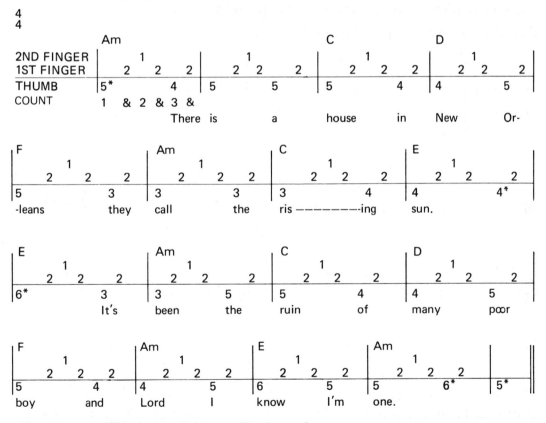

* These notes are 'fill-ins', not melody notes. Play them softer.

Melody notes which are not in the chords can be played with this pattern by taking a finger off a chord, or putting a finger on another string—as they were in Brush Stroke playing on pages 57-59.

A few different notes are needed for the tune which follows. Notes which are not in the chords, or have been changed, are marked with a small number next to the string number. This small number gives the fret at which the note is to be played—

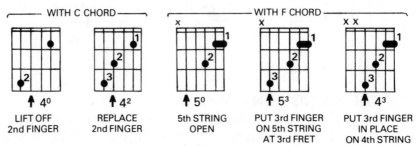

| WITH C CHORD | | WITH F CHORD | | |
|---|---|---|---|---|
| ↑ 4⁰ | ↑ 4² | ↑ 5⁰ | ↑ 5³ | ↑ 4³ |
| LIFT OFF 2nd FINGER | REPLACE 2nd FINGER | 5th STRING OPEN | PUT 3rd FINGER ON 5th STRING AT 3rd FRET | PUT 3rd FINGER IN PLACE ON 4th STRING |

Before you play the tune, practise the last two Bars of the 3rd line until you can play them smoothly. The pattern here, and in the last Bar of the 1st line is played by the thumb and 1st finger only.

## PLAISIR D'AMOUR by Martini il Tedesco

Important melody notes are underlined. Play them a little more strongly so they stand out from the backing.

# More Advanced Music

In many tunes you will find notes which last for less than one beat—

♪ is an Eighth Note. In most music it lasts for half a beat.
You have already played Eighth Notes in Fingerpicking and Brush Strokes —they are the notes counted by putting '&' between each beat.

♬ is a Sixteenth Note. It lasts for half as long as an Eighth Note.
Sixteenth Notes are best counted by dividing each beat into four parts, and counting like this: <u>1</u> ² ³ ⁴ <u>2</u> ² ³ ⁴ <u>3</u> ² ³ ⁴ <u>4</u> ² ³ ⁴

Eighth Notes and Sixteenth Notes are often found joined to other Eighth Notes or Sixteenth Notes—

TWO EIGHTH NOTES  TWO SIXTEENTH NOTES  ONE EIGHTH NOTE  TWO SIXTEENTH NOTES

Count Eighth Notes and Sixteenth Notes like this—

Tap your foot for the underlined beats only.

### MORE 'DOTTED' NOTES
Reminder—A dot after a note makes it last half as long again.
Dotted Quarter Notes and Dotted Eighth Notes are counted like this—

Count and play all the examples on this page—all notes are on open strings. For rhythm and melody playing with a plectrum, use down-strokes and upstrokes to play Eighth Notes and Sixteenth Notes—

## RESTS

In most music one or more of the players or singers is silent for a few beats. These silent beats are called 'Rests'. Rests are counted in exactly the same way as notes—

You can stop the strings of your guitar sounding for Rests, and at the end of tunes, by lightly touching them with the edge of your right hand.

## MORE TIME SIGNATURES

You may find $\frac{2}{4}$ and $\frac{6}{8}$ Time Signatures in some music. When you do, count the beats for them like this—

In some tunes, the first and last Bars do not have the full number of beats given by the Time Signature. This happens because the tune starts in the middle or at the end of the first Bar. In these tunes, count the missing beats before you begin playing, to get the timing right.

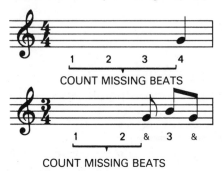

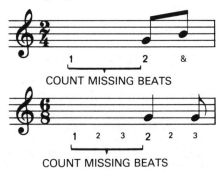

Counting out the 'timing' is the secret to finding out how long each note or Rest should last to make the music sound right. Try counting and playing all examples shown here, before going on to the tunes on the next page. Always start counting slowly and evenly, so you understand the rhythm and melody, before trying to play at the correct speed. If a few notes or chords seem to slow up your playing, practise them on their own until you can play them at the same speed as the rest of the tune. Come back to these pages, and pages 40 and 45, if ever you are uncertain about the timing of any notes, Rests or Time Signatures.

**CLEMENTINE**—an American folk song.
This tune starts at the end of the first Bar. Count the missing beats to lead you in, then follow the counting for the Eighth Notes and Rests. When you have played the melody, try singing or humming the tune to the 3 beat Brush Stroke backings shown on pages 51 or 54.

**SILENT NIGHT**—a Christmas song from Austria.
Play the melody to this tune, following the counting. At the very end you will find a 'Tied Note'. (See page 45 if you have forgotten what this means.) Then, sing the melody and play a fingerpicking backing with the pattern and Bass Notes you learned on page 64. Play the pattern once for each Bar, and change chords where the chord names are marked.

69

# Sharps (♯) and Flats (♭)

So far the music in this book has been written with what are called 'Natural Notes'—A, B, C, D, E, F and G. The Natural Notes you have played are all shown together on this diagram of the fingerboard—

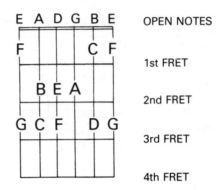

On the fingerboard, there are gaps where other notes can be played. These other notes are called 'Sharps' and 'Flats' and they are found between most of the Natural Notes. As you can see on the diagram, there is no gap for a Sharp or Flat Note between B and C or between E and F, but there are places for Sharps and Flats between all the other notes.

## SHARPS (♯)

A Sharp Note is one fret position higher than the plain Natural Note with the same letter name. 'F Sharp' is played on the 1st string behind the 2nd fret, one fret higher than the plain F (Natural) Note—

Sharp Notes are marked with a Sharp Sign—♯. (F Sharp is written F♯). On the Stave, Sharp Notes are shown with a Sharp Sign (♯) in front of the note which is to be 'sharpened'.

70

## FLATS (♭)

A Flat Note is one fret position *lower* than the plain 'Natural Note' with the same letter name. 'G Flat' is one fret lower than G (Natural)—

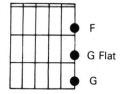

Flat Notes are marked with a Flat Sign—♭. (G Flat is written G♭.) On the Stave, Flat Notes are shown with a Flat Sign (♭) in front of the note which is to be 'flattened'.

| A | A♭ | G | G♭ | F | E | E♭ | D | D♭ | C | B | B♭ | A |
|---|----|---|----|---|---|----|---|----|---|---|----|---|

NO FLAT NOTE HERE          NO FLAT NOTE HERE

As you can see, F Sharp is the same note as G Flat, on the guitar. In fact, all of these notes can have either a Sharp or Flat name—

A♯ = B♭     C♯ = D♭     D♯ = E♭     F♯ = G♭     G♯ = A♭

As well as changing the notes marked by them, ♯ and ♭ signs also affect notes in the same position on the Stave which follow in the Bar—

E     F♯     ALSO F♯                    B     B♭     ALSO B♭

However, if the note is to be Sharp or Flat again in the next Bar, the Sharp or Flat Sign will be used again.

## NATURAL SIGNS (♮)

A Sharp or Flat can be cancelled by a 'Natural Sign' (♮). Written in front of a note, it tells us the Natural Note is needed instead of a Sharp or Flat which was marked earlier. This sign also affects all notes in the same position which follow in the Bar.

F♯     F(NATURAL)     ALSO
                      F NATURAL

Two Sharp Notes are needed for the next tune—

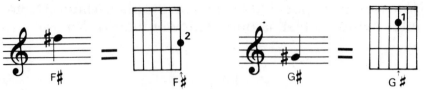

## GREENSLEEVES—an old English love song.
This melody is also used for the Christmas Carol 'What Child is This?'.

The notes marked '(♯)' are also G Sharp notes, because the Sharp Sign in front of the first 'G' affects all G notes which follow in the Bar. The notes marked '(♮)' are plain 'G Naturals' played on the 3rd string open, because there is no Sharp Sign in front of them.

After playing the melody, play a fingerpicking backing with the pattern and Bass Notes shown on page 64. Play the pattern once for each Bar.

# Notes up to the 4th fret

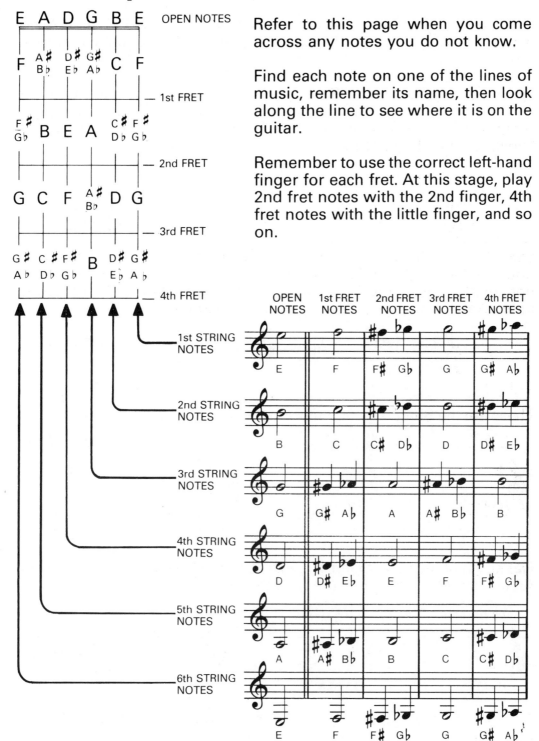

Refer to this page when you come across any notes you do not know.

Find each note on one of the lines of music, remember its name, then look along the line to see where it is on the guitar.

Remember to use the correct left-hand finger for each fret. At this stage, play 2nd fret notes with the 2nd finger, 4th fret notes with the little finger, and so on.

# Music in different Keys

Until now, all music in this book has been in the Keys of 'C' or 'A Minor', with C Chords, A Minor Chords and other chords normally found with them.

When you play music in different Keys, with different sets of chords, you will find Sharp and Flat Signs used in another way. These Sharp and Flat Signs appear immediately after the Clef on every line of music in what are known as 'Key Signatures'.

Each Sharp or Flat Sign of the Key Signature is written in the position of a note. It affects ALL NOTES in the music which have the same name as the note marked. Here, the Sharp Sign is in the position of an 'F' note (shown in brackets). It means EVERY F must be 'sharpened'—

These are the Sharp Key Signatures which you are most likely to find:

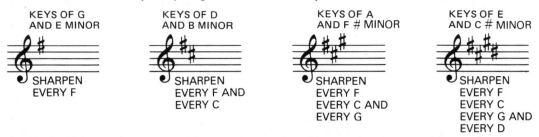

| KEYS OF G AND E MINOR | KEYS OF D AND B MINOR | KEYS OF A AND F # MINOR | KEYS OF E AND C # MINOR |
|---|---|---|---|
| SHARPEN EVERY F | SHARPEN EVERY F AND EVERY C | SHARPEN EVERY F EVERY C AND EVERY G | SHARPEN EVERY F EVERY C EVERY G AND EVERY D |

Flat Key Signatures are similar. Each Flat Sign is in the position of a note. All notes with the same name must be 'flattened'.

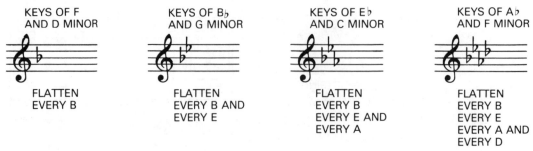

| KEYS OF F AND D MINOR | KEYS OF B♭ AND G MINOR | KEYS OF E♭ AND C MINOR | KEYS OF A♭ AND F MINOR |
|---|---|---|---|
| FLATTEN EVERY B | FLATTEN EVERY B AND EVERY E | FLATTEN EVERY B EVERY E AND EVERY A | FLATTEN EVERY B EVERY E EVERY A AND EVERY D |

Different Keys enable us to play different combinations of chords and melody notes to make music more interesting. They also enable us to play higher or lower to suit different instruments and voices.

Play the Scales of the Keys of G and F and hear the difference.
In the Scale of G, F♯ is played instead of F (Natural).
In the scale of F, B♭ is played instead of B (Natural). Play B♭ on the 3rd string with the 3rd finger behind the 3rd fret.

SCALE OF G (One Sharp)                    SCALE OF F (One Flat)

The notes of the scale and other notes with the same names, are the melody notes you can expect to find in music in each Key.

Extra ♯ , ♭ or ♮ signs may be found in music in any Key. Remember they also affect notes in the same position which follow in the Bar.

**BOOGIE IN G**—F♯ is in the Key Signature.

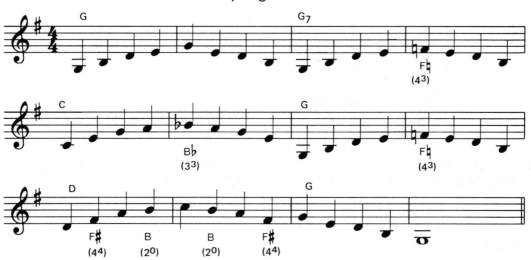

F♮ (4³) = 4th string, 3rd fret.   B♭ (3³) = 3rd string, 3rd fret.   B (2⁰) = 2nd string open.
F♯ (4⁴) = 4th string, 4th fret—play with 4th finger.

Look up on page 73 any notes which you may have forgotten.

Take care to read Sharps, Flats and Naturals correctly, or your music will not sound right. Read these pages again if you have any doubts about Sharps, Flats, Naturals or Key Signatures.

# More Fingerpicking

We now come to what are probably the best-known and most popular types of Fingerpicking—the styles which are often called 'Clawhammer'. These all rely on a strong regular thumb pattern over which the fingers pick out a different interweaving pattern, or the melody. The whole secret to these styles is keeping a steady thumb rhythm going regardless of what the fingers do. Start slowly and count evenly. Learn to play each pattern smoothly and correctly before going on to the next.

First let us establish a steady thumb pattern—it is the same as some you have already played. Put your right hand in place with the thumb resting on the 5th string and the 1st finger on the 1st string. Finger a C Chord and play the thumb pattern on its own—

$\frac{4}{4}$    C

| THUMB STRINGS | 5 | 3 | 5 | 3 | 5 | 3 | 5 | 3 | 5 | 3 | 5 | 3 |
|---|---|---|---|---|---|---|---|---|---|---|---|---|
| COUNT | 1 | 2 | 3 | 4 | 1 | 2 | 3 | 4 | 1 | 2 | 3 | 4 |

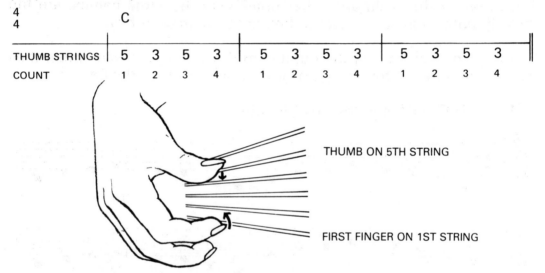

THUMB ON 5TH STRING

FIRST FINGER ON 1ST STRING

In the next stage, the thumb and 1st finger gently pluck at the same time in a 'pinching' movement, every time you count '1'—

$\frac{4}{4}$    C

| 1ST FINGER STRING | 1 | | | | 1 | | | | 1 | | | |
|---|---|---|---|---|---|---|---|---|---|---|---|---|
| THUMB STRINGS | 5 | 3 | 5 | 3 | 5 | 3 | 5 | 3 | 5 | 3 | 5 | 3 |
| COUNT | 1 | 2 | 3 | 4 | 1 | 2 | 3 | 4 | 1 | 2 | 3 | 4 |

Now count "1—2—3 and 4" and pluck with the 1st finger on 'and' as well as on '1'.

$\frac{4}{4}$    C

| 1ST FINGER STRING | 1 | | 1 | | 1 | | 1 | | 1 | | 1 | |
|---|---|---|---|---|---|---|---|---|---|---|---|---|
| THUMB STRINGS | 5 | 3 | 5 | 3 | 5 | 3 | 5 | 3 | 5 | 3 | 5 | 3 |
| COUNT | 1 | 2 | 3 & 4 | | 1 | 2 | 3 & 4 | | 1 | 2 | 3 & 4 | |

Finally, the 1st finger plays a pattern on the 1st *and* 2nd strings—

$\frac{4}{4}$

| | C | | | | C | | | | G₇ | | | | C |
|---|---|---|---|---|---|---|---|---|---|---|---|---|---|
| 1ST FINGER STRINGS | 1 | | 2 | | 1 | | 2 | | 1 | | 2 | | 1 |
| THUMB STRINGS | 5 | 3 | 5 | 3 | 5 | 3 | 5 | 3 | 6 | 4 | 6 | 4 | 5 |
| COUNT | 1 | 2 | 3 | & 4 | 1 | 2 | 3 | & 4 | 1 | 2 | 3 | & 4 | 1 |

You have just learned an important melody pattern for Fingerpicking. Make sure you can play it smoothly and correctly before continuing.

Melodies are played on the 1st, 2nd and 3rd strings with notes from the chords, or by taking a finger off or adding a finger to chords. Try finding the notes shown here—with the correct fingering! Then play them with the pattern. Move your fingers at dotted-lines and Bar-Lines.

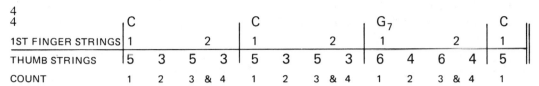

G    G₇    G₆    MODIFIED G    C    ALTERNATIVE C    C

$\frac{4}{4}$

| | | | | | | | | | | | |
|---|---|---|---|---|---|---|---|---|---|---|---|
| 1st Finger Strings | 1⁽³⁾ | | 1⁽¹⁾ | 1⁰ | | 2³ | 2⁽¹⁾ | | 1³ | | 1⁽⁰⁾ |
| Thumb Strings | 6 | 3 | 6 | 3 | 6 | 3 | 6 | 3 | 5 | 3 | 5 | 3 | 5 |

When you can play smoothly, try the melody pattern with this tune—

**SKIP TO MY LOU**—Fingerpicking melody playing.

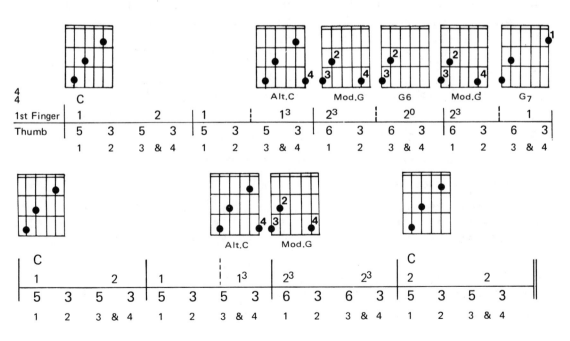

$\frac{4}{4}$

| | C | | | | Alt.C | | Mod.G | | G6 | | Mod.G | | G7 | |
|---|---|---|---|---|---|---|---|---|---|---|---|---|---|---|
| 1st Finger | 1 | | 2 | | 1 | 1³ | 2³ | | 2⁰ | 2³ | | 1 | |
| Thumb | 5 | 3 | 5 | 3 | 5 | 3 | 5 | 3 | 6 | 3 | 6 | 3 | 6 | 3 | 6 | 3 |
| | 1 | 2 | 3 | & 4 | 1 | 2 | 3 | & 4 | 1 | 2 | 3 | & 4 | 1 | 2 | 3 | & 4 |

Alt.C    Mod.G    C

| | C | | | | | 1³ | 2³ | | 2³ | C | | | |
|---|---|---|---|---|---|---|---|---|---|---|---|---|---|
| 1 | | 2 | | 1 | | 1³ | 2³ | | 2³ | 2 | | 2 | |
| 5 | 3 | 5 | 3 | 5 | 3 | 5 | 3 | 6 | 3 | 6 | 3 | 5 | 3 | 5 | 3 |
| 1 | 2 | 3 | & 4 | 1 | 2 | 3 | & 4 | 1 | 2 | 3 | & 4 | 1 | 2 | 3 | & 4 |

77

Another popular Fingerpicking pattern for melody playing has an extra note played by the 1st finger. Count it 1   2 & 3 & 4. Notes which fall on the underlined beats should be played stronger.

| 4/4 | | C | | | | C | | | | G₇ | | | | C | |
|---|---|---|---|---|---|---|---|---|---|---|---|---|---|---|---|
| **1ST FINGER** | | 1 | | 1 | 2 | 1 | | 1 | 2 | 1 | | 1 | 2 | 1 | |
| **THUMB** | | 5 | 3 | 5 | 3 | 5 | 3 | 5 | 3 | 6 | 4 | 6 | 4 | 5 | |
| **COUNT** | | 1 | 2 & | 3 & | 4 | 1 | 2 & | 3 & | 4 | 1 | 2 & | 3 & | 4 | 1 | |

The melody of the next tune is played with this pattern. Look through all the diagrams and practise the *exact* fingering, before playing it.

## BANKS OF THE OHIO—Fingerpicking Guitar Solo.

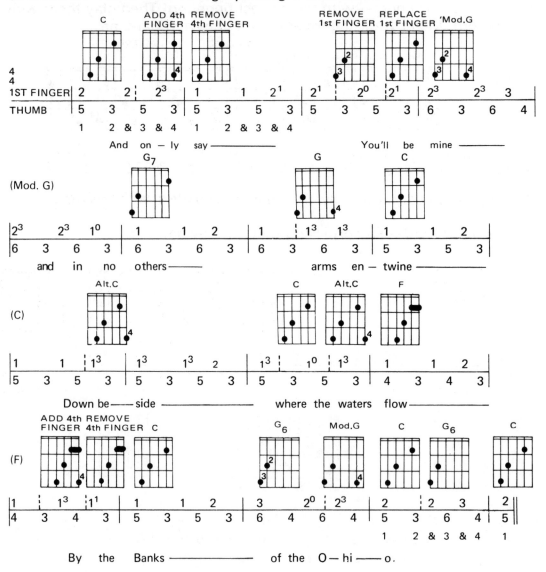

The pattern on the facing page can be used for playing many melodies. Tunes which do not fit it exactly often work out if the 1st finger notes are put in different places—on the beat with the thumb notes or between the beats. Otherwise some notes can be left out.

The same pattern can also be played with the 1st and 2nd fingers for backings, as shown below. Start with the 1st finger on the 2nd string, and the 2nd finger on the 1st string. Play the first Bar several times to practise the finger movements, before playing different chords. In the second Bar of the second line, the fingers move to the 2nd and 3rd strings with the thumb plucking different Bass Notes—Fingerpicking can often be varied by moving the fingers to other strings.

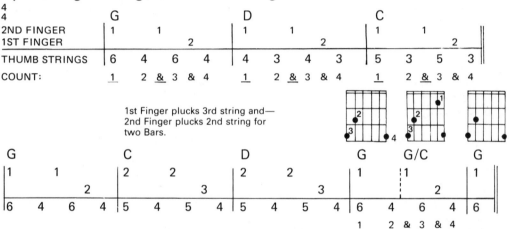

| 4/4 | | G | | | | D | | | | C | | | |
|---|---|---|---|---|---|---|---|---|---|---|---|---|---|
| 2ND FINGER | | 1 | | 1 | | 1 | | 1 | | 1 | | 1 | |
| 1ST FINGER | | | | | 2 | | | | 2 | | | | 2 |
| THUMB STRINGS | | 6 | 4 | 6 | 4 | 4 | 3 | 4 | 3 | 5 | 3 | 5 | 3 |
| COUNT: | | 1 | 2 & | 3 & | 4 | 1 | 2 & | 3 & | 4 | 1 | 2 & | 3 & | 4 |

1st Finger plucks 3rd string and— 2nd Finger plucks 2nd string for two Bars.

| | G | | | | C | | | | D | | | | G | | G/C | | G | |
|---|---|---|---|---|---|---|---|---|---|---|---|---|---|---|---|---|---|---|---|
| | 1 | | 1 | | 2 | | 2 | | 2 | | 2 | | 1 | | 1 | | 1 | |
| | | | | 2 | | | 3 | | | | 3 | | | | | 2 | | |
| | 6 | 4 | 6 | 4 | 5 | 4 | 5 | 4 | 5 | 4 | 5 | 4 | 6 | 4 | 6 | 4 | 6 | |
| | | | | | | | | | | | | | 1 | | 2 & | 3 & | 4 | |

Add an extra note, played by the 1st finger, and you have another very popular fingerpicking backing pattern. Practise the first Bar several times before playing with different chords. Count 1 & 2 & 3 & 4—

| 4/4 | C | | | | F | | | | G | | | | C |
|---|---|---|---|---|---|---|---|---|---|---|---|---|---|
| 2nd Finger Strings | 1 | | 1 | | 1 | | 1 | | 1 | | 1 | | 1 |
| 1st Finger Strings | | 2 | | 2 | | 2 | | 2 | | 2 | | 2 | 2 |
| Thumb Strings | 5 | 3 | 5 | 3 | 4 | 3 | 4 | 3 | 6 | 4 | 6 | 4 | 5 |
| Count: | 1 & | 2 & | 3 & | 4 | 1 & | 2 & | 3 & | 4 | 1 & | 2 & | 3 & | 4 | 1 |

Play this pattern as a backing for tunes which have 4 beats to the Bar. (4/4 or **C** Time Signatures.)

The fingerpicking patterns and other techniques you have learned form the basis of many different Folk, Ragtime, Country and Blues styles of playing. Go on and have fun with Fingerpicking.

More Fingerpicking patterns and tunes to play, along with other styles are to be found in Roger Evans' book *Fingerstyles for the Guitar*, published by EMI Music Publishing.

# How to play with a Capo

A 'Capo'—or 'Capotasto'—is a handy gadget which allows the same chord shapes to be used for playing in different Keys. It is very useful for the Flamenco, Folk, Blues and Fingerpicking guitarist, as it enables these styles to be played in Keys which would otherwise be extremely difficult. Play these styles with a 'Capo' if you want your backings or solos to sound in higher Keys for singing or for different effects. However, do not let the Capo become a substitute for learning new chords or other left-hand techniques.

The Capo is clamped just behind a fret to press the strings firmly on to the fingerboard. The higher up the neck it is placed, the higher each note or chord sounds.

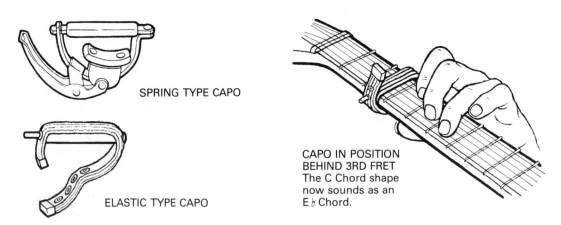

SPRING TYPE CAPO

ELASTIC TYPE CAPO

CAPO IN POSITION
BEHIND 3RD FRET
The C Chord shape
now sounds as an
E♭ Chord.

Various types of Capos are sold in music shops, but the most popular are those shown here. Spring Capos are easy to move up and down the neck. However, Elastic Capos are preferred by many players because they are lighter and less cumbersome. Thicker Elastic Capos are made specially for steel-strung guitars. If your guitar has a curved fingerboard, you will get the best results with Capos which have a slightly curved bar. (The bar or rod of a capo can be bent a little at a time into a gentle curve in a vice, if the plastic or rubber covering is removed. Replace the covering after bending the bar or rod.)

Tune your guitar before putting on a Capo. Press the bar of the Capo on to the strings just behind a fret with your right hand, and clip it together with the left hand. Make sure it is parallel to the fret. The Capo should be just tight enough to get a clear sound from each string. (Squeeze a Spring Capo while you put it in place. With Elastic Capos, hold the bar in place with the long end of the elastic at the bottom. Then pull the elastic around the back of the neck and hook the first hole on to the rod. Play each string. If any do not sound clearly, hook the second hole on to the rod. Do not tighten an Elastic Capo any more than necessary, or it will wear out quickly.)

When the Capo is in place, play a chord to check that the guitar is still in tune. (If necessary, adjust the tuning with the Capo on, by counting the frets up from it to compare the strings. After re-tuning, slacken the Capo to release any tension and check the tuning again. This way the guitar should be in tune when you next move the Capo.)

Always slacken the Capo before moving it to another fret. Sliding it along the strings will wear it out, and may pull the strings out of tune.

If a song is too high or too low for singing, try the Capo behind different frets—move it up two or three frets at a time until you reach the right Key. If you do not find a suitable Key, 'transpose' the backing to another Key as explained on page 106. Also try Fingerpicking and Brush Strokes with the Capo behind various frets.

## CHORD AND NOTE NAMES AT DIFFERENT CAPO POSITIONS

The name of each chord or note changes when played with the Capo behind different frets. Find the name of a chord or note on the top line of the chart, and look down the column to find its new name at each Capo position. Look up Minor, 7th and other chords under their letter names— they become Minors, 7ths, etc. in new Keys with the Capo. For example, the Am Chord becomes 'Cm' with the Capo at the 3rd fret, G7 becomes Bb7 with the Capo at the 3rd fret, and so on.

| WITHOUT CAPO | A | A#Bb | B | C | C#Db | D | D#Eb | E | F | F#Gb | G | G#Ab |
|---|---|---|---|---|---|---|---|---|---|---|---|---|
| CAPO AT 1ST FRET | A#Bb | B | C | C#Db | D | D#Eb | E | F | F#Gb | G | G#Ab | A |
| CAPO AT 2nd FRET | B | C | C#Db | D | D#Eb | E | F | F#Gb | G | G#Ab | A | A#Bb |
| CAPO AT 3rd FRET | C | C#Db | D | D#Eb | E | F | F#Gb | G | G#Ab | A | A#Bb | B |
| CAPO AT 4th FRET | C#Db | D | D#Eb | E | F | F#Gb | G | G#Ab | A | A#Bb | B | C |
| CAPO AT 5th FRET | D | D#Eb | E | F | F#Gb | G | G#Ab | A | A#Bb | B | C | C#Db |
| CAPO AT 6th FRET | D#Eb | E | F | F#Gb | G | G#Ab | A | A#Bb | B | C | C#Db | D |
| CAPO AT 7th FRET | E | F | F#Gb | G | G#Ab | A | A#Bb | B | C | C#Db | D | D#Eb |

# Useful Left-Hand Techniques

### HAMMERING-ON
'Hammering-on' allows extra notes to be played by pushing a string sharply onto a higher fret after it has been plucked.

Try this. Play the 3rd string open. While it is still sounding, and without plucking it again, 'hammer' the string on to the fingerboard behind the 2nd fret with your left-hand 2nd finger. Another note should sound clearly. Now, pluck the 3rd string again and 'hammer' it on to the fingerboard behind the 3rd fret with your 3rd finger, for another note.

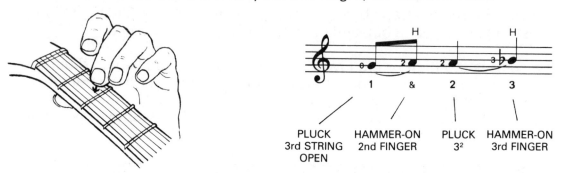

In Guitar Music, 'Hammering-on' is shown by an upward curved line between the two notes, or a letter 'H' over the second note. In 'Classical' style playing, it is called an 'Ascending Ligado'.

### PULLING-OFF
In 'Pulling-off', left-hand fingers 'pluck' extra notes.
Try this—Play the 1st string with your 3rd finger behind the 3rd fret. While the string is still sounding, pull the 3rd finger slightly across and off the string, so the open note is heard.

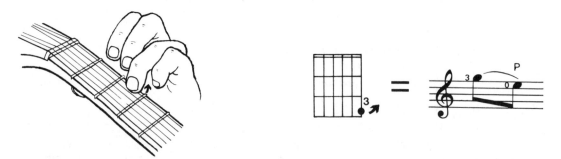

In Guitar Music, 'Pulling-off' is shown by a downward curved line between the two notes, or·a letter 'P' over the second note. In 'Classical' style playing, it is called a 'Descending Ligado'.

Try hammering-on and pulling-off together—

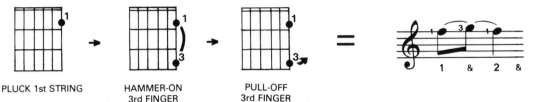

PLUCK 1st STRING     HAMMER-ON     PULL-OFF
                 3rd FINGER     3rd FINGER

Make very definite left-hand finger movements. Even though the string is plucked just once, you should hear three equally loud clear notes.

Hammering-on and pulling-off enable fast runs of notes to be played smoothly. Melody notes which do not fit Fingerpicking patterns can often be played by hammering-on or pulling-off. In Brush Stroke playing, notes played by the thumb or plectrum can be hammered-on.

### SLIDING NOTES
Sliding Notes are used for Lead and melody playing. A note is fingered by the left hand and played. While it is still sounding, the finger slides firmly up or down the string to play another note—
Put the left-hand 2nd finger on the 3rd string behind the 1st fret. Pluck the 3rd string, then slide the finger up to the 2nd fret, so another note is sounded. Then try it in reverse—

In Guitar music, this is shown with a straight line between the notes.

### BENDING NOTES
This technique is used in Blues, Jazz and Rock music, to make a whining sound, and play what are called 'Blue Notes'.

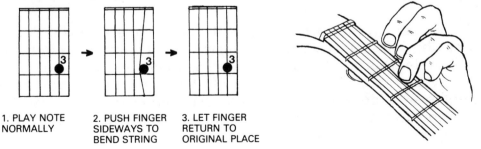

1. PLAY NOTE     2. PUSH FINGER     3. LET FINGER
NORMALLY          SIDEWAYS TO       RETURN TO
                  BEND STRING       ORIGINAL PLACE

# Some 'Classical' Guitar Techniques

Many of the techniques of 'Classical' style guitar playing are similar to those you have already learned. However, some other basic techniques should be practised before attempting this style of playing —

### PLUCKED CHORDS

Three or four strings are often plucked together to sound a chord. This is similar to what you have already learned, except that the thumb and two or three fingers pluck at the same time.

Finger a C Chord. Then, position your right hand as shown here —

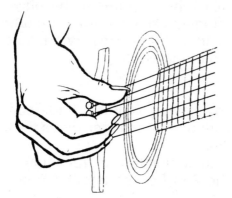

THUMB ON 5TH STRING

1ST FINGER ON 3RD STRING
2ND FINGER ON 2ND STRING
3RD FINGER ON 1ST STRING

Clench your fingers and thumb slightly, so they pluck all four strings evenly at the same time. (Make sure the 1st string sounds clearly.) After plucking, the fingers and thumb should be just clear of the strings, until they are ready to pluck again. Now try playing this —

|  | C | G7 | C |
|---|---|---|---|
| 3RD FINGER STRING | 1 | 1 | 1 |
| 2ND FINGER STRING | 2 | 2 | 2 |
| 1ST FINGER STRING | 3 | 3 | 3 |
| THUMB STRING | 5 | 6 | 5 |

Practise plucking different chords, making sure each string sounds equally loud and clear.

On the Stave, notes which are played at the same time as a chord, are shown one above the other. In Guitar Music a small number is often put in front of a note. This number gives the *left-hand finger* which should be used to play the note. Read the notes of chords exactly as you read melody notes — decide where each note is on the fingerboard and use the left-hand finger indicated by the number in front of the note to play it — '1' = 1st finger, '2' = 2nd finger, '0' = Open string, and so on.

84

A three note chord is similar, but plucked by two fingers and the thumb. Here, a separate Bass Note is played by the thumb between each chord. (The finger notes last two beats, the thumb notes last one beat.)

| | C | | | |
|---|---|---|---|---|
| 2nd FINGER STRING | 1 | | 1 | |
| 1st FINGER STRING | 2 | | 2 | |
| THUMB STRINGS | 5 | 3 | 5 | 3 |

Here the finger notes last one beat, the thumb notes last two beats—

| | C | | | |
|---|---|---|---|---|
| 2nd FINGER STRING | 1 | 1 | 1 | 1 |
| 1st FINGER STRING | 2 | 2 | 2 | 2 |
| THUMB STRINGS | 5 | | 3 | |

In these two examples, the notes played by the thumb are shown with their 'stems' pointing down, while the finger notes have their 'stems' pointing up. Guitar Music is often written this way when notes played by the thumb, or fingers have a different 'timing' from other notes.

## ARPEGGIOS

An 'Arpeggio' is a chord with the notes sounded one after the other. (Arpeggio comes from the Italian name for a harp, which gives an idea of the effect.) Position your right hand as for 'Plucked Chords' and pluck each string separately and evenly, starting with the thumb—

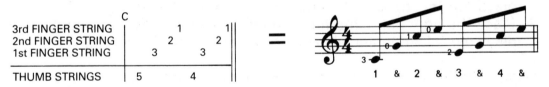

Another type of 'Arpeggio' goes up and then down again—

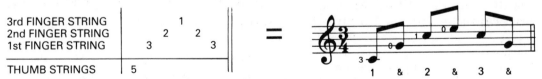

Play each of these arpeggios several times to practise them.

You should learn to recognise the way Chords and Arpeggios are written on the Stave if you wish to read music for 'Classical' and some other styles of guitar playing. Read each note of the examples on these pages while you play them, to practise reading guitar music.

## THE REST STROKE

The Rest Stroke, which is also called the 'Apoyando' in 'Classical' playing and the 'Picardo' in Flamenco, is probably the single most important technique for solo guitar playing in these styles. It is used for playing fast runs of notes and for making the important notes of melodies stand out, particularly on the 1st, 2nd and 3rd strings.

A Rest Stroke is played like this—
Place the right-hand 1st finger under the 1st string, keeping the other fingers just off the strings. Bend the 1st finger slightly, so it plays the 1st string *and comes to rest on the 2nd string*.

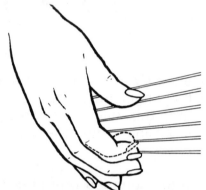

1ST FINGER PLAYS
1ST STRING AND COMES
TO REST ON THE 2ND STRING.

Rest Strokes are frequently played by alternating the 1st and 2nd fingers on the same string, like this—
1. Place the right-hand 1st finger on the 1st string, bend it slightly so it plays the 1st string and comes to rest on the 2nd string.
2. Place the right-hand 2nd finger on the 1st string, bend it slightly so it plays the 1st string and also comes to rest on the 2nd string.

Now, play the same again. This time, when the 2nd finger starts to bend, lift the 1st finger off the 2nd string and move it down to play the 1st string again. As the 1st finger comes up, move the 2nd finger down, and so on. (Your fingers should appear as though they are walking.) Now play several notes on the 1st string by alternating the 1st and 2nd fingers—

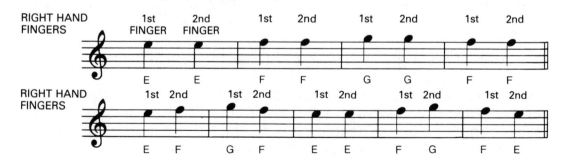

86

Practise Rest Strokes on all strings by playing notes at each fret. (See 'Training Your Fingers' on page 26.) Play each note with a different *right-hand* finger—Play one note with the 1st finger, the next note with the 2nd finger, the next note with the 1st finger, and so on. Also try alternating the 1st, 2nd *and 3rd* fingers to play notes.

## FREE STROKES

'Free Stroke' is the name given to thumb or finger plucking which does not come to rest on a string. (The fingers play 'Free Strokes' in Finger-picking.) Free Strokes are used for Chords, Arpeggios and melody notes which do not need the strength of Rest Strokes. Go over the tunes you have learned, and play Rest Strokes for notes which you feel should be strong, and play Free Strokes for the other notes.

In the next tune, the thumb part is shown with the stems of the notes pointing down. Follow the left-hand fingering given by the numbers in front of notes, and remember that the Key Signature sharpens every F. Notice that the 1st and 3rd lines are exactly the same.

**MINUET IN G** by Bach.

# How to become a better guitarist

By the time you reach this part of the book, you should be on the way to becoming a good guitarist—as long as you have learned to play each technique and piece of music correctly before going on to the next. Before going any further, return to anything you did not understand and read it again. Go back to any music or technique which you found at all difficult and try it again. The secret to becoming a really good player is to take the trouble to keep practising each technique a little at a time until it becomes completely natural.

You are at a very important stage. You know quite a lot about playing the guitar and have learned the basic techniques of most styles of playing. Now is the time to polish your playing, and make the most of what you have learned by playing new pieces of music.

From here on, there are new techniques and friendly advice to help you become an even better guitarist.

## POLISH YOUR PLAYING
Always try to make your music flow. Pick or pluck the strings smoothly so each note sounds loudly and clearly. Practise right-hand techniques until you can play evenly, smoothly, and naturally, without thinking about what you are doing.

After playing each note, keep your left-hand finger in place on a string until you are ready to play the next note. 'Walk' your left-hand fingers from one note to the next, so there are no gaps between notes.

Try playing with your eyes closed and let your ears tell you whether your fingers are in the right places. This will help you to feel more confident and natural with your guitar, and make it easier for you to read music without looking at your fingers all the time.

## READ MUSIC AS OFTEN AS POSSIBLE
The more you read music, the easier it becomes, so practise reading music whenever you can. Look for new music to read, it does not have to be guitar music—anything with the 𝄞 Clef will do. Read music for the recorder and other instruments, look for books of Folk Songs in your library, and so on. Every new tune will help you learn to read more quickly and play better. Choose simple music at first—tunes which are not too long, without too many Sharps or Flats in the Key Signature. Look up any notes you may have forgotten on page 73 or page 92.

## PRACTICE

Continue to follow the Practising Plan on page 37. Every week try to learn something new, or really polish something you are still learning. Set aside a few minutes everytime you play to go over anything which you find at all difficult.

## LEARN FROM OTHER GUITARISTS

Listen to guitar music as often as you can—on records, and on radio and television. Listen closely to all types of music and different styles of playing, and try to imagine how you would play them.

Go out and watch other people playing, preferably in places where you can get close enough to see what a guitarist is doing. The players do not have to be 'big-name performers'—you can learn a lot from anyone who plays in public, as long as you remember the basic rules and do not pick up another guitarist's bad habits. If you see a technique which interests you, try playing it yourself when you get home.

You can often meet other guitarists at small informal folk, blues or jazz clubs, or at a guitar society. Most guitarists are normally pleased to talk about their music, and may even show you a trick or two, but do not ask too much at one time—no one wants to give away all of their secrets. However, concerts are not a good place to try and talk to musicians, because there are usually too many people around.

## DO YOU NEED GUITAR LESSONS?

If you are happy with what you play, or if you are a 'natural guitarist' who finds learning easy, you may manage without guitar lessons for a while, provided you play enough different music and learn from other players. However, lessons are almost essential if you want to play 'Classical', Flamenco or Jazz, or take other guitar styles seriously. A good teacher will help you progress far more quickly than you could on your own. He or she will suggest suitable music for you, explain how different techniques are played, and help you in many other ways.

If you want to take lessons, choose a teacher who is expert in the music you would like to play. Your music shop or a guitar society may be able to recommend someone and give you an idea of the cost of lessons, otherwise, look for advertisements for guitar lessons in local newspapers or music magazines. Talk to the teacher about your standard of playing and what you would like to learn, before committing yourself to a series of lessons, and consider whether you would prefer individual lessons, or tuition in a class.

# Playing higher up the Fingerboard

So far you have been playing at what is called the '1st position'—with your left-hand 1st finger playing notes at the 1st fret. (Each position is named after the fret where the 1st finger plays.) At the 1st position, you can play notes on any strings up to the 4th fret, if you use all of your left-hand fingers. Notes higher than these are played by moving the left hand to higher fret positions.

At the other positions you will find new higher sounding notes, along with notes which you have played on other strings. At the 5th position (with the 1st finger behind the 5th fret and the thumb underneath it), you will find some higher notes—A, B and C—along with the notes E, F and G *on the 2nd string*. These notes on the 2nd string are the *same* notes you played on the 1st string at the 1st position! Higher up still, you will find these same notes repeated on the 3rd string at the 9th position—

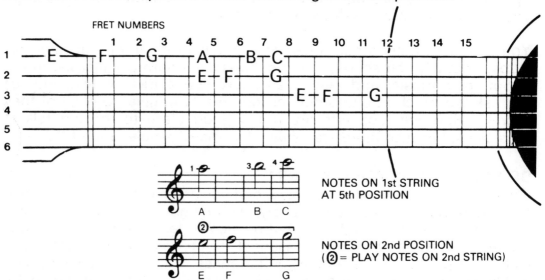

NOTES ON 1st STRING
AT 5th POSITION

NOTES ON 2nd POSITION
(②= PLAY NOTES ON 2nd STRING)

Notes above the Stave are written with 'Leger Lines'. 'A' is on the first Leger Line, 'B' is in the space above, and so on. In Guitar Music, a circled number over a note gives the string on which it is to be played, if it is not obvious: ② = play this note on the 2nd string.

The new higher notes are important, but the other notes are also very useful, even though they can be played at lower frets. Imagine a tune which has 'C' on the 1st string behind the 8th fret as its highest note, and 'F' as its lowest note. Playing 'C' with the 3rd finger on the 1st string and 'F' with the 1st finger on the 2nd string at the 6th fret, is easier than moving the whole left hand up and down the neck. Try it both ways!

Higher up the fingerboard, the strings have a different tone and the spaces between the frets are narrower, which suits Lead Guitar playing. Play the notes E, F and G on the 1st string, then on the 2nd string at the 5th position and on the 3rd string at the 9th position, and compare the different tone of the notes on each string. If you want an even tone, you should try to play whole tunes around the same position. (As an aid to playing, the 5th, 7th, 9th and 12th positions are marked with dots on the edge of the fingerboard on many guitars.)

## HOW TO WORK OUT NOTES HIGHER UP THE FINGERBOARD

Think back to how you tune your guitar, and you will realise you know some of the notes higher up the fingerboard—the 2nd string at the 5th fret is the same as the 1st string open (the note E), the 3rd string at the 4th fret is the same as the 2nd string open (B) and so on. The notes at the 12th fret are another reference point—the note on each string at the 12th fret has the same name as the open string, but it is eight notes—an 'Octave' —higher. The note on the 3rd string at the 12th fret is called 'G' just like the open note, but it is a higher G—the same note as the 1st string at the 3rd fret.

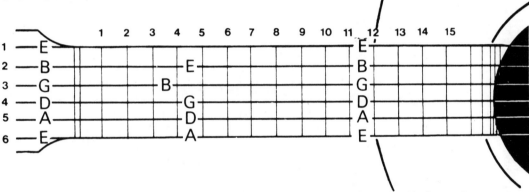

Use these notes as a reference, and you can work out all the other notes by going up or down one fret at a time—as long as you remember where the Sharps and Flats occur. (There are no Sharps or Flats between E and F, or between B and C, but there are Sharps and Flats between all the other notes.)

Try working out some notes for yourself on the guitar and write their names in pencil on the chart. Then check yourself by looking up the notes on the next page.

Read the music to tunes and scales and play them at higher positions, and you will come to know where each note is found higher up the fingerboard. It is normally best to choose positions where you can play the highest note with the 3rd or 4th finger of your left hand.

# All Notes on the Guitar

All the notes normally played on the guitar are shown here, so you can use this chart to look up any notes you do not know. Notice that a separate Stave is used here for notes on each string. Find any note you do not know on one of the Staves, and look up the column to the same string on the guitar diagram to see where the note is played.

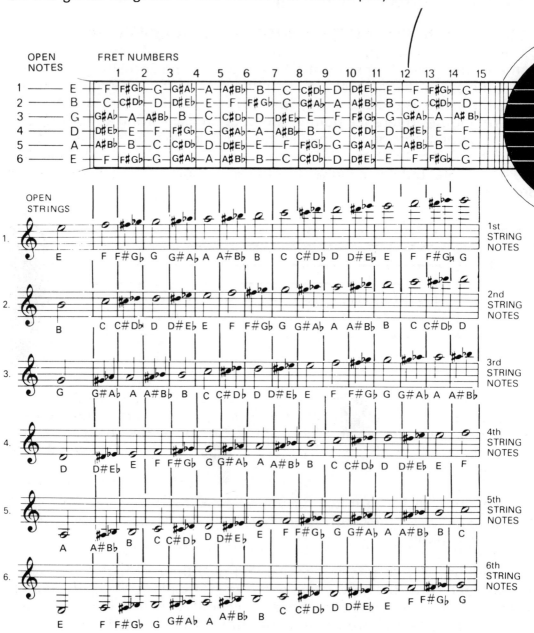

# Chords for every Key

In the next few pages you will find a good selection of chords for every Key. It is not essential to learn all of these chords, as you can look them up when you come across them in music. However, go through all of the chords a few at a time, making sure you use the correct fingering, so you will know how to play them. Practise these important chords: A, A7, A°, A+, B♭, B♭m, B♭7, Bm7, C7, D7, F7 and Fm.

In these pages, the following signs and abbreviations are used—

| | |
|---|---|
| Alt. | An Alternative chord shape. Some of these chords are easier, some are more interesting or give a better sound. |
| ° or dim. | Diminished Chords. (C° or C dim is short for C Diminished.) Each diminished chord can be named after any of the four different notes it contains—C° is also E♭°, A° and F♯°. |
| + or aug. | Augmented Chords. (A+ or A aug. is short for A Augmented.) Each augmented chord can be named after any of the three different notes it contains—A+ is also C♯+ and F♯+ |
| maj. 7 | Major 7th Chord. These should not be confused with the normal '7' or 'm7' chords as they are used differently. |
| sus 4,<br>7 sus 4 | Suspended Chords. May also be written 'sus.' or '7sus.' |
| C/D or<br>C (D Bass) | Chords like these are sometimes found in Sheet Music. The chord is changed so it has a different Bass Note— C/D is a C Chord with D as the Bass Note. |
| III, IV | Roman numerals mark the fret behind which the 1st finger is positioned if chords are to be played above the 1st position on the fingerboard—III = 3rd fret, IV = 4th fret, and so on. |
| × | The string or strings marked with '×' should not sound. Strings can often be deadened by touching them lightly with the nearest finger when playing chords. |
| N | 'Name' note of the chord. If on the 3rd, 4th, 5th or 6th strings, this is the main Bass Note for the chord. |
| * | Chords marked * may also be played at other positions on the fingerboard—as long as no open strings are allowed to sound. (See page 97.) |

Chords played *with* open strings are called 'Open Chords'.
Chords played *without* any open strings are called 'Closed Chords'.

Both the Sharp and Flat names for chords are shown here, although such names as 'A Sharp', 'D Flat', 'D Sharp' and 'G Flat' are rarely used.

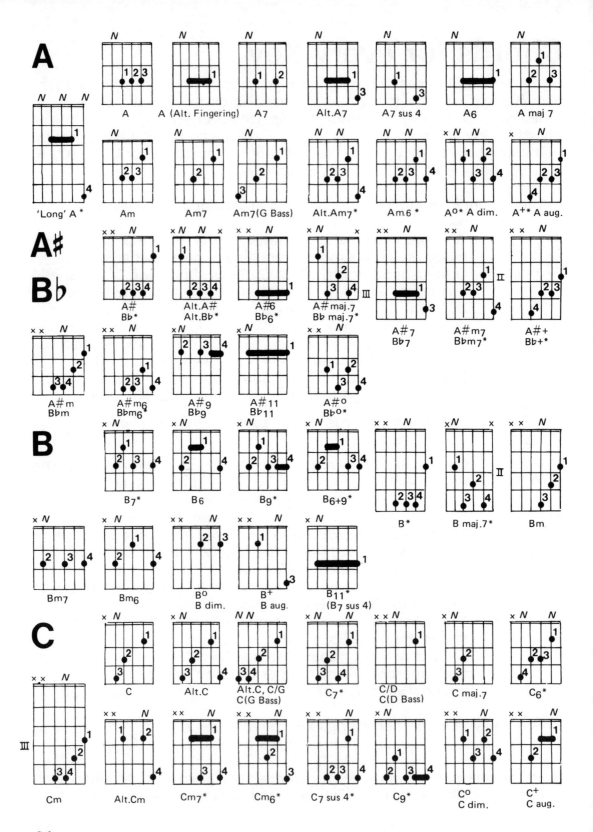

94

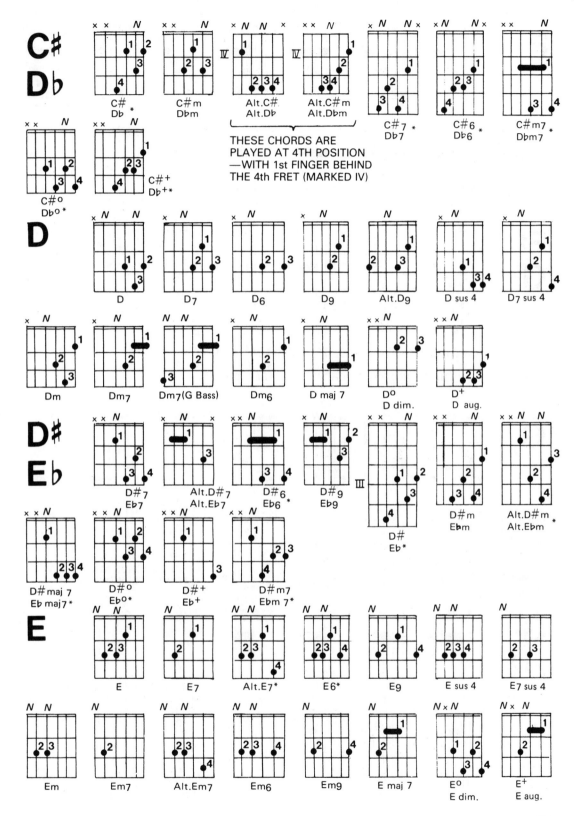

C#
Db

C#
Db *

C#m
Dbm

Alt.C#
Alt.Db

Alt.C#m
Alt.Dbm

C#7 *
Db7

C#6 *
Db6

C#m7 *
Dbm7

C#o
Dbo *

C#+
Db+*

THESE CHORDS ARE
PLAYED AT 4TH POSITION
—WITH 1st FINGER BEHIND
THE 4th FRET (MARKED IV)

D

D

D7

D6

D9

Alt.D9

D sus 4

D7 sus 4

Dm

Dm7

Dm7(G Bass)

Dm6

D maj 7

Do
D dim.

D+
D aug.

D#
Eb

D#7
Eb7

Alt.D#7
Alt.Eb7

D#6
Eb6 *

D#9
Eb9

D#
Eb*

D#m
Ebm

Alt.D#m
Alt.Ebm *

D# maj 7
Eb maj7 *

D#o
Ebo*

D#+
Eb+

D#m7
Ebm 7*

E

E

E7

Alt.E7*

E6*

E9

E sus 4

E7 sus 4

Em

Em7

Alt.Em7

Em6

Em9

E maj 7

Eo
E dim.

E+
E aug.

95

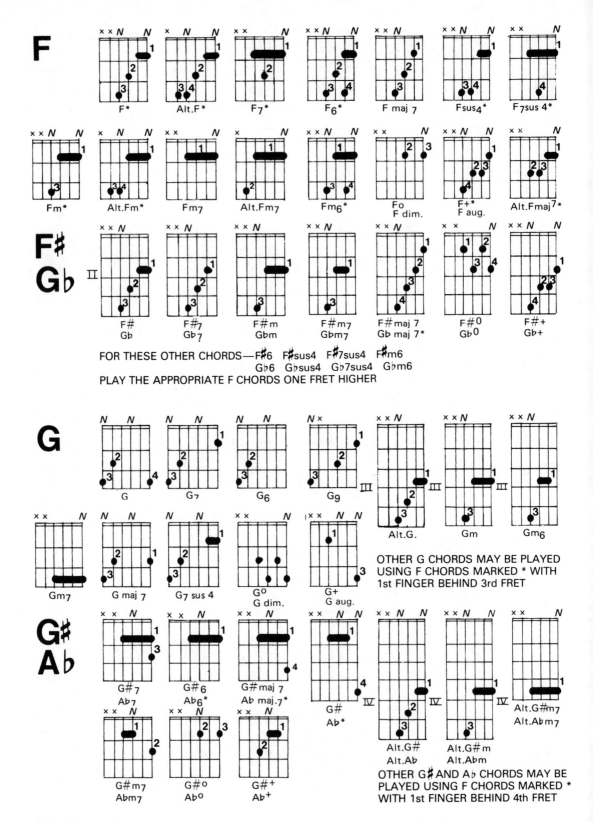

**F**

F* Alt.F* F₇* F₆* F maj 7 Fsus4* F₇sus 4*

Fm* Alt.Fm* Fm₇ Alt.Fm₇ Fm₆* Fo / F dim. F+* / F aug. Alt.Fmaj7*

**F♯ / G♭**

F♯ / G♭  F♯₇ / G♭₇  F♯m / G♭m  F♯m₇ / G♭m₇  F♯ maj 7 / G♭ maj 7*  F♯⁰ / G♭⁰  F♯+ / G♭+

FOR THESE OTHER CHORDS—F♯6  F♯sus4  F♯7sus4  F♯m6
Gb6  Gbsus4  Gb7sus4  Gbm6
PLAY THE APPROPRIATE F CHORDS ONE FRET HIGHER

**G**

G  G₇  G₆  G₉  Alt.G.  Gm  Gm₆

Gm₇  G maj 7  G₇ sus 4  G⁰ / G dim.  G+ / G aug.

OTHER G CHORDS MAY BE PLAYED
USING F CHORDS MARKED * WITH
1st FINGER BEHIND 3rd FRET

**G♯ / A♭**

G♯₇ / Ab₇  G♯₆ / Ab₆*  G♯ maj 7 / Ab maj.7*  G♯ / Ab*  Alt.G♯ / Alt.Ab  Alt.G♯ m / Alt.Abm  Alt.G♯m₇ / Alt.Abm₇

G♯m₇ / Abm₇  G♯⁰ / Ab⁰  G♯+ / Ab+

OTHER G♯ AND A♭ CHORDS MAY BE
PLAYED USING F CHORDS MARKED * 
WITH 1st FINGER BEHIND 4th FRET

# Chords higher up the Fingerboard

Each of the useful chord shapes marked * in the previous pages can be played at different positions to make chords for any Key—*as long as no open strings are allowed to sound*. The F Chord is one of the basic 'Closed Chord' shapes. Moved to the 2nd position (with the 1st finger behind the 2nd fret), it becomes an F♯ Chord. At the 3rd position, it becomes a G Chord, and so on. Other F Chords, like F7, F6 and Fm work in the same way—at the 2nd position they become F♯7, F♯6 and F♯m; at the 3rd position they become G7, G6 and Gm, and so on.

Although not strictly a Closed Chord, C7 can be used as one if the 1st and 6th strings are 'deadened' by touching them lightly with the 1st and 3rd fingers. This very useful chord becomes C♯7 at the 2nd position, D7 at the 3rd position, E♭7 at the 4th position, and so on.

You can work out the name of each Closed Chord at different positions from the notes marked '*N*' on the chord diagrams on the previous pages. For example, C7 is named after the notes played on the 2nd and 5th strings. Move the C7 shape to the 3rd position and the notes on these strings become 'D'—and you have a D7 Chord.

Try working out the names of Closed Chords at different positions and play them with new tunes and tunes you already know. (If you are not certain about the names of notes at different frets, look them up on the Fingerboard diagram on page 92.) The following chord shapes are very useful—F and Alt. F, Fm and Alt. Fm, B♭, B♭7, B♭m, C7 and C♯. Within a few frets, these shapes will make the chords for most tunes in any Key. Try the F shape as a C Chord, the B♭ shape as an F Chord and the C7 shape as a G7 Chord to play a backing at the 8th position.

Generally, it is best not to mix Open and Closed Chords, or move up and down the fingerboard very much, so choose chords which are around the same position for a balanced rhythmic sound.

## DAMPING CHORDS

Different rhythm effects can be made by relaxing the left hand a little to 'damp' a chord after it has been played. Try this effect with Closed Chords, and with these Open Chords—D, Dm, Dm7, A, Am and E. After 'damping', press the strings before playing the chord again.

# The Barré or Bar

The Barré or Bar is a technique which gives full six string chords for every Key. The left-hand first finger forms a 'Bar' across all six strings behind a fret. Other fingers are then added to make up a complete chord. Make a six string Barré Chord like this:

1. Lay the left-hand first finger across all the strings just behind the 1st fret.
2. Put the thumb lightly in position in the middle of the neck underneath the 1st fret.
3. Put the other fingers in place as shown below in the diagram.
4. Press the thumb against the back of the neck and play the chord. The thumb should press just hard enough to make a clear sounding chord, but no harder. Relax your hand, then try again.

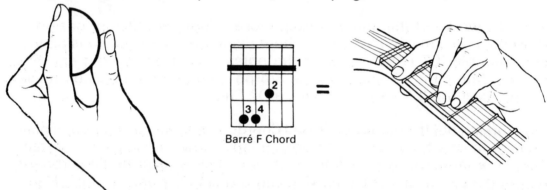

Barré F Chord

Practise this a little every day with your 1st finger behind different frets until each note of the chord sounds clearly in all positions. Never press harder than necessary or you will tire your hand. If any strings do not sound clearly, check that *all* your fingers are correctly positioned. The Barré is normally awkward at first, but it will come with regular practice, if you are patient.

A 'Half-Barré' by the 1st finger covers only three or four strings. It is used in solo playing for notes which are on different strings at the same fret. A Half-Barré is also used to play F Minor and other chords.

In Guitar Music, a Barré is marked by a letter 'C' followed by a Roman Numeral for the fret where it is to be played—CIV = play a Barré with the 1st finger behind the 4th fret.
A Half-Barré is marked ¢. ¢V = Play a Half-Barré with the 1st finger covering three or four strings behind the 5th fret.
If a line follows the Barré sign, (CIII————,) the Barré should be held until the end of the line.

The Barré works like a moveable 'Capo' above which Open Chord shapes can be played—if the fingering is altered so the chord is played without the 1st finger. The Barré chord on the facing page is really an E Chord shape played with the 1st finger acting as a Capo behind the 1st fret. All Barré chords are similarly based on Open Chord shapes. They can all be played at every fret position to make chords for any Key—

BASED ON OPEN E CHORD SHAPES    BASED ON OPEN A CHORD SHAPES    BASED ON D7 CHORD

BARRÉ CHORDS

(1)  (2)  (3)  (4)  (5)  (6)  (7)

| NAME AT 1st POSITION | F | $F_7$ | Fm | A# or Bb | A#$_7$ or Bb$_7$ | A#m or Bbm | (5 STRINGS) D#$_7$ or Eb$_7$ |
|---|---|---|---|---|---|---|---|
| 2nd POSITION | F# or Gb | F#$_7$ or Gb$_7$ | F#m or Gbm | B | B$_7$ | Bm | E$_7$ |
| 3rd POSITION | G | G$_7$ | Gm | C | C$_7$ | Cm | F$_7$ |
| 4th POSITION | G# or Ab | G#$_7$ or Ab$_7$ | G#m or Abm | C# or Db | C#$_7$ or Db$_7$ | C#m or Dbm | F#$_7$ or Gb$_7$ |
| 5th POSITION | A | A$_7$ | Am | D | D$_7$ | Dm | G$_7$ |
| 6th POSITION | A# or Bb | A#$_7$ or Bb$_7$ | A#m or Bbm | D# or Eb | D#$_7$ or Eb$_7$ | D#m or Ebm | G#$_7$ or Ab$_7$ |
| 7th POSITION | B | B$_7$ | Bm | E | E$_7$ | Em | A$_7$ |
| 8th POSITION | C | C$_7$ | Cm | F | F$_7$ | Fm | A#$_7$ or Bb$_7$ |
| 9th POSITION | C# or Db | C#$_7$ or Db$_7$ | C#m or Dbm | F# or Gb | F#$_7$ or Gb$_7$ | F#m or Gbm | B$_7$ |
| 10th POSITION | D | D$_7$ | Dm | G | G$_7$ | Gm | C$_7$ |

These seven chords may be used to play many different tunes in any Key.

It is normally best to play around the same part of the fingerboard—if you want to play in Eb (with chord number 4 at the 6th position), choose the Barré shapes which give other chords around the same position—play chord number 1 at the 4th position as an Ab Chord, chord number 2 at the 6th position as a Bb7 Chord, and so on. Try using Barré chords in this way for tunes you know. Mix Closed Chords with Barré Chords occasionally to give your hand a rest.

Other Barré Chords can be made up with five or six string Open Chord shapes. E and A chord shapes are best, but some D, C and G chord shapes can be used if you have long fingers. The names of Barré Chords at different positions can be worked out from the name notes which are marked 'N' on the chord diagrams on this page and pages 94–96.

# Learning to play new music

Now is the time for you to gain experience by learning to play many different pieces of music. The easiest way to learn, is to buy printed music for tunes you like, or borrow it from a library. Look for 'Albums' which contain several tunes as they are normally far better value than the 'Sheet Music' for a single tune. Your music shop should have albums of 'Easy Guitar' arrangements in which you will probably find some tunes which you would like to play.

Start with short, simple pieces of music, preferably tunes you know well which are not too fast. Avoid music with more than four ♯s or ♭s in the Key Signature as the melody will be more difficult to read, and the chords may not be easy. When you have learned to play a few 'easy' tunes, try tunes which are longer, or tunes in different Keys with different chords. Always try to learn something new from each piece of music.

Take each tune in easy stages. Learn one thing at a time—work out what the left hand must do, before you try anything complicated with the right hand.

If you are playing the melody or a guitar solo, see which Sharps or Flats are in the Key Signature, and remember that they affect *every* note with the same name. Work out where all the notes are on the guitar—before worrying about their timing. Add variety to your playing by plucking the strings in different places—nearer the bridge for a brighter tone, or in the middle of the soundhole for a mellow tone.

If you are playing a backing, practise the chord changes by playing each chord once only, before trying to play a full rhythm or finger-picking backing. (The backing should have the same number of beats as the Time Signature: $\frac{3}{4}$ = 3 beats, **C** or $\frac{4}{4}$ = 4 beats, and so on.) Sing or hum the tune while you are playing the backing chords.

See if any part of the music is repeated, as this can save you the trouble of working out everything more than once. (See 'How to read Sheet Music' on pages 102—103 for signs which mean the music is repeated.) Learn to play each piece of music properly before going on to something new, or you may end up knowing how to play parts of several tunes without being able to play any of them completely. If any tune does not sound right when you play it, check that you are reading the music correctly and following any Sharp, Flat or Natural Signs. Make sure you always use the right fingering for chords, and change them at the correct times.

# Learning new songs

The easiest way to learn songs is from printed music which gives the melody, chords and lyrics (words). As with everything else, it is best to learn one thing at a time, so approach new songs in simple steps—

1. Play the melody, or the first part of it, and sing the song to find out if the music is in the right Key for you. If it is too high or too low, use a Capo or change the music to another Key (see page 106).

2. Go through all of the chords to make sure you know them all, and practise any chord changes which are new to you.

3. Play the first few notes of the melody to lead you in. Then sing the song, while you play the first chord in each Bar. This will help you learn how to sing the song and understand its feeling.

4. Try different rhythms with the chords until you find the right backing for the song. (Speaking the words of a song out loud often gives an idea of the rhythm to use.) Then, practise playing and singing together. The lyrics of songs are often easier to remember if you write them out for yourself, instead of reading them from the music.

Keep your backings simple so you can concentrate on singing rather than playing. Avoid complicated chord changes or difficult right-hand patterns which may interrupt the flow of the words of the song, or make it sound stilted. Even if you are accompanying another singer, keep the backing subdued so it does not overwhelm the song. The backing should always suit the feeling of a song—use bright backings for happy songs and gentle backings for quiet songs. Bass Notes played with Brush Strokes or a simple Fingerpicking pattern often make very attractive backings, particularly if the spaces between the lyrics are filled-in with extra notes or runs to make the song more interesting. Use the 'name' note of each chord as the main Bass Note, and pick another note from the chord for other Bass Notes.

Work out a good beginning and ending for each song. Play the first few chords or make-up an 'introduction' based on the first part of the melody to lead you in. To finish, continue the backing for the number of beats shown in the music and build up the song to a definite ending. Listen to records and hear how other players start and finish tunes, and how they fill-in the gaps between verses. However, do not always copy the way everyone else sings or plays. Make up your own versions sometimes, keeping within the feeling of the music.

# How to read Sheet Music

The music in most 'Albums' and 'Sheet Music' is written so it can be used for singing and for playing on many different musical instruments, so you need to know which parts to read for the guitar. The first Bars of a typical piece of Sheet Music normally look somewhat like this, with the melody line shown over the piano or organ part—

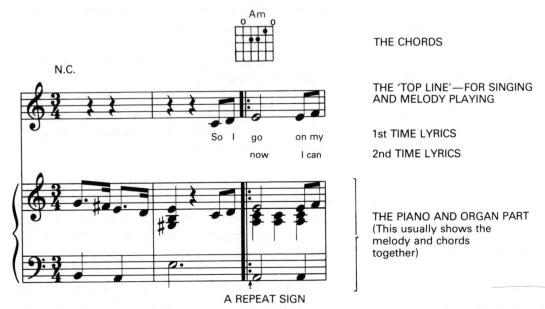

THE CHORDS

THE 'TOP LINE'—FOR SINGING AND MELODY PLAYING

1st TIME LYRICS

2nd TIME LYRICS

THE PIANO AND ORGAN PART
(This usually shows the melody and chords together)

A REPEAT SIGN

The 'Top Line' will interest you most if you are a singer or Lead Guitarist, because this is the melody of the music. Underneath are the lyrics (words) of a song. Each word is shown underneath the melody notes to which it is sung. The top set of words are sung for the first verse, any other lyrics are sung when the tune is repeated.

The chord names and suggested chord shapes for the tune are usually shown over the Top Line. Some chord shapes may have a small 'o' over one or more of the strings. This means the strings marked 'o' are to be played open—*but any other open strings should not be played*. The chord shapes given in Sheet Music do not always give a full sound, so it is often better to choose other chord shapes which have the same name. 'N.C.' means no chord is to be played for this part of the music.

If there seem to be too many chord changes in a Bar of music, try playing just the first chord in each Bar, and leave out the others. If this does not sound right, try playing the chords which fall on the 1st and 3rd beats. If this does not work either, you should play all of the chords to give a proper backing to a tune.

In Sheet Music, various signs are used if parts of the music are to be played more than once. Make sure you understand how these signs work in each piece of music before you start to play it.

REPEAT SIGN. This means go back to a similar sign — and repeat the music in between. If there is no other sign, repeat the music from the beginning.

FIRST and SECOND TIME SIGNS. The first time through, the music includes the part marked ⌐1 ⌐. Second time around, this part is left out and replaced by the music marked ⌐2

D.C.    'D.C.' or 'Da Capo' means repeat from the beginning.

D.S. 𝄋    This means 'Go back to the sign — 𝄋 —and repeat the music until
al ⊕'Coda  you come to 'to Coda ⊕', then go to the music marked 'Coda ⊕'.

The order in which the music is to be played is often obvious in songs from the way the lyrics (words) are written.

In some tunes, the melody is changed slightly for the second or third verses. These changes are often shown with smaller than normal notes—

2nd VERSE MELODY
(SMALL NOTES)

1st VERSE MELODY

(1) When      I'm     not      with      you
(2) now that  I'm     com—ing  home to   you

## MAKING UP 'INTROS' AND GUITAR SOLOS FROM PIANO PARTS

Many players completely disregard the Piano Part of Sheet Music, but it can be very useful and interesting for the guitarist.

In many tunes, the first few notes of the piano part can be used as an 'Introduction' to lead you into the tune, particularly if these notes start before the melody, as in the example opposite. The whole piano part can also be made into a guitar solo with some tunes. To do this, try playing most of the upper line of the piano part, adding the Bass Notes you would normally play with the chords of the tune—or better still, play notes with the same names as the Bass Notes shown on the bottom line of the piano part, if you know how to read them.

*How To Read Music*, another book by Roger Evans, explains other words, signs, and notes which you may find in music.

# Reading Guitar Music

Music which is arranged for the guitar often includes signs which explain how the music should be played. The usual signs are shown here—

 Numbers in front of notes refer to the left-hand fingers which are to play the notes. 1 = 1st finger, 2 = 2nd finger, 3 = 3rd finger, 4 = 4th finger and 0 = Open string note.
Notes which are one above the other are played as a chord.

 ②③etc. Circled numbers give the strings on which notes are played. (② = 2nd string) If followed by a line: ②———, all notes are to be played on that string until the end of the line.

⑥—D This means the 6th string is to be tuned to D. See page 122.

Right-hand fingers which are to be used to play notes—

p i m a    p = thumb, i = index (1st) finger, m = middle (2nd) finger, a = annular or ring (3rd) finger, (Spanish method.)

T I M R    T = Thumb, I = Index (1st) finger, M = Middle (2nd) finger, R = Ring (3rd) finger. (Fingerpicking and Tablature method.)

⊓   V    ⊓ = Play note with a downstroke (↓). V = Upstroke (↑)
The V sign is sometimes used to indicate 'Rest Strokes'.

𝕮   𝕮̸    𝕮 = Barré or Bar, 𝕮̸ = Half-Barré. See page 98.

II III IV    Roman numerals give the fret position of the 1st finger.
5th pos.    The 1st finger is positioned behind the 5th fret, etc.

 The letters 'H' or 'P', or curved lines between two notes indicate 'Hammering-on' or 'Pulling-off'. See page 82.

A straight line between notes means they are played by sliding one finger up or down the string. See page 83.

har.12    Harmonic to be played at fret indicated. See page 120.

Note: Music for the guitar is written an 'Octave' higher than it sounds—

 in guitar music is the same note as ♪♭ in music for other instruments. However, this does not normally affect guitar playing, as music for most instruments can be played exactly as it is written.

# How to read Tablature

Tablature is an alternative way in which guitar music may be written. It is always marked 'TAB' or 'T' to distinguish it from standard music. Tablature uses SIX lines—one for each string of the guitar—

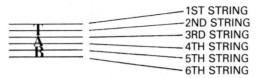

Numbers on the string lines give the *FRETS* at which each string is to be played: 1 = 1st fret, 2 = 2nd fret, 0 = Open String, and so on.

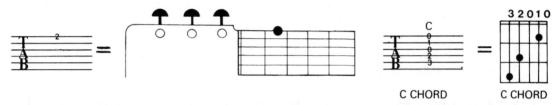

Tablature is straightforward to read. Simply play the strings which have a number on them—with your left-hand fingers behind the frets indicated by the numbers.

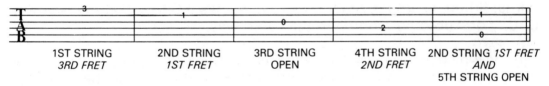

| 1ST STRING | 2ND STRING | 3RD STRING | 4TH STRING | 2ND STRING *1ST FRET* |
|---|---|---|---|---|
| *3RD FRET* | *1ST FRET* | OPEN | *2ND FRET* | *AND* 5TH STRING OPEN |

The right-hand patterns are usually similar to those you have learned— The 1st and 2nd fingers normally play the 1st, 2nd or 3rd strings with the thumb adding Bass Notes on the 3rd, 4th, 5th or 6th strings.
The 'T I M R' right-hand method (see facing page) may also be used—

Two forms of Tablature are shown here. On the right, the length of each note is shown by adding a 'stem' to the number—Here, Quarter Notes (♩) and Eighth Notes (♪) are shown. Other musical signs may also be added, along with 'H' for Hammering-on, 'P' for Pulling-off, 's' for Sliding Notes and 'b' for Bending Notes. (See pages 82 and 83.)

# Changing music to other keys

With the notes you have learned, and the chords shown in this book, you can play in any Key. However, some Keys are better than others for individual singing voices, and for certain styles of playing—and music is not always written in these Keys. When you come across music which is too high or too low for singing, or in a Key which does not suit your style of playing, you can change it to another Key with the chart shown here. This is called 'Transposing' music to another Key.

**HOW TO TRANSPOSE CHORDS TO ANOTHER KEY**
1. Find the Key of the music. The Key usually has the same name as the chord with which the music finishes. (In the example shown below, the last chord is E♭, and the Key is E♭.) You can also use the Key Signature as a guide to the Key—see page 74.

2. Find the Key in the left column of the chart and lay a pencil under it to act as a marker.

3. Choose a new Key. (C or Am, G or Em all give simple open chords.)

4. Find the name of the first chord of the music on the line of the chart marked by the pencil. Then, look up or down that column to the new Key, read off the new name for the chord, and write it over the original chord name. (In the example, the E♭ Chord becomes a C Chord in the new Key of C.) Look up other chords in the same way.

Chords which are Minors, 7ths, 6ths, etc. in the original Key must become Minors, 7ths, 6ths, and so on in the new Key. (In the example, C *Minor* becomes A *Minor, Fm7* becomes *Dm7* and B♭7 becomes *G7*.) If the new Key is not right for playing or singing, choose another Key.

AN EXAMPLE IN TWO KEYS
1. Original Key—E♭

2. New Key—C

| KEY | 1 | | 2 | | 3 | 4 | | 5 | | 6 | | 7 |
|---|---|---|---|---|---|---|---|---|---|---|---|---|
| | | | | | | | | NUMBER OF NOTE IN MAJOR SCALE | | | | |
| A♭ or Fm | A♭ | A♮ | B♭ | B♮ | C | D♭ | D♮ | E♭ | E♮ | F | F♯ G♭ | G |
| A or F♯m | A | A♯ B♭ | B | C♮ | C♯ | D | D♯ E♭ | E | F♮ | F♯ | G♮ | G♯ |
| B♭ or Gm | B♭ | B♮ | C | C♯ D♭ | D | E♭ | E♮ | F | F♯ G♭ | G | G♯ A♭ | A |
| C or Am | C | C♯ D♭ | D | D♯ E♭ | E | F | F♯ G♭ | G | G♯ A♭ | A | A♯ B♭ | B |
| D or Bm | D | D♯ E♭ | E | F♮ | F♯ | G | G♯ A♭ | A | A♯ B♭ | B | C♮ | C♯ |
| E♭ or Cm | E♭ | E♮ | F | F♯ G♭ | G | A♭ | A♮ | B♭ | B♮ | C | C♯ D♭ | D |
| E or C♯m | E | F♮ | F♯ | G♮ | G♯ | A | A♯ B♭ | B | C♮ | C♯ | D♮ | D♯ |
| F or Dm | F | F♯ G♭ | G | G♯ A♭ | A | B♭ | B♮ | C | C♯ D♭ | D | D♯ E♭ | E |
| G or Em | G | G♯ A♭ | A | A♯ B♭ | B | C | C♯ D♭ | D | D♯ E♭ | E | F♮ | F♯ |

DISREGARD NATURAL SIGNS ( ♮ ) FOR CHORDS.   KEYS NOT NORMALLY USED ARE NOT SHOWN.

## TRANSPOSING MELODIES

This takes a little longer, but is worthwhile for a good piece of music. You will need some manuscript paper printed with the five lines of the Stave—or draw your own lines on a piece of paper.

1. Find the Key of the music (as explained for Transposing Chords) and lay a pencil on the chart as a marker. Then choose a new Key.

2. Read the music one note at a time. Look up each note on the line of the chart for the original Key. Then follow the column up or down to the new Key. Read off the note and write it on the manuscript. Make sure the melody line is similar in both Keys—it should go up and down in the new Key exactly as it did in the original Key.

The notes of the Scales of Major Keys are shown larger on the Chart. These are the notes you are most likely to find in music in each Key. (Remember that the ♯ and ♭ signs of Key Signatures affect all notes with the same names.) Look up any notes you may have forgotten on page 92.

Any ♯, ♭ or ♮ notes not in the Key Signature will need to be written in the music where they occur. Look up these notes in the original Key and follow the column up or down to find the note names in the new Key.

Follow these instructions carefully and transpose the example shown at the bottom of the facing page, before trying your own music.

# Playing by ear

Playing by ear is easier than you might think—if you do not try to play complicated music too soon. Like everything else, the secret is to learn to do it in easy stages.

Start with a tune you have already played, so you are playing partly from memory and partly by ear. It should be a tune you know well enough to sing or hum, but one which you could not play without reading the music. Anything will do, as long as it is short and simple, with no Sharps or Flats to complicate it. (Try any of the tunes in this book up to page 69, unless you remember them all completely.)

Read and play the first few notes to start you off, and sing or hum the whole tune several times until you are completely sure of it. Then, put the music away. Now play the first few notes again and try to find the next note. If the melody goes up, try notes which are higher. If the melody goes down, try lower notes. Keep trying different notes (No Sharps or Flats) until you have the next note in the tune. Then look for the note which follows, and so on.

If you lose the tune, go back and play it again from the beginning. (It may help you to write down each note as you find it.) As long as you can manage to work out just two or three notes by yourself, you are well on the way to playing by ear. When you have worked out one tune, you will find other tunes easier, as long as you pick music you know very well, so you can tell when you are playing the right notes.

Chord backings can also be worked out 'by ear'. Once again it is best to start with tunes which you know well enough to sing. Choose a short tune which has C as the first chord.

Play a C Chord slowly, one string at a time. Then sing the melody in tune with the chord. (If you have trouble doing this, play the first few notes of the melody to lead you in.) Keep playing the chord and singing the melody, until the chord clashes with your singing. Then, try other chords which you think may fit. (G7 or F are the most likely.)

When you have found the right chord, play and sing the tune again from the beginning, changing to the new chord where it fits the tune. Continue singing and playing with this new chord until it too clashes with your singing. Then try other chords which you think might fit. (The third chord in the tune could well be a C Chord again.) Then, go on and work out the other chord changes in the same way.

Work out the rhythm, by tapping your foot evenly in time with your singing and playing—1 2 3 4 1 2 3 4, and so on. If the tune fits, you can work out a proper backing. If it does not fit, try a 3 beat rhythm—1 2 3 1 2 3. Most tunes fit one or other of these patterns. (You will find that most chord changes take place on the first beat of a rhythm—when you count '1'—but sometimes you will find chord changes on the third beat as well.)

If what you have worked out sounds right, it probably is right, but check by looking at the music. If you have difficulty remembering the chord changes, write the chord names over the words of a song.

Next try an *easy* tune which you have not played, but which you know very well. (How about 'Jingle Bells' or 'Happy Birthday to You'?)

First the melody. Play a C Chord slowly, one string at a time, and sing the first few notes of the melody in tune with the chord. Now, find the first note of the melody on your guitar. (It will usually be one of the notes of the C Chord.) Then find the next note, and the note after that, and so on. Music in the Key of C usually has no Sharps or Flats, so look first for the melody among the 'Natural Notes'. (In case you find it hard to start, the first notes of 'Jingle Bells' are EEE, EEE, EGCDE—start on the 1st string. The first notes of 'Happy Birthday to You' are GGAGCB—starting on the 3rd string.)

When you have worked out the melody, try working out the chords and rhythm as explained earlier. When you have done this, check the chords you have chosen by looking at the bottom of the next page.

After some experience playing by ear and from music, you will begin to recognise the chord and melody patterns which fit most tunes. Start playing by ear in 'C' as this is the easiest Key to work in. C, F and G7 chords are most common in the Key of C, but other chords such as Am, Dm, D and Em can occur, along with chords which you might not expect at all. If you have difficulty in finding a chord to fit, work out the melody notes at that point in the tune, and try chords which contain those notes. Remember that tunes in the Key of C will normally end on a C Chord.

When you have worked out tunes in C, you can change them to other Keys by 'Transposing' or by playing the notes of another chord to start you off, but remember that other Keys will include Sharps and Flats.

If C is not the right Key for a particular song, use a Capo or try starting in the Key of G with a G Chord. If the tune has a 'minor' feeling, try Am or Em as the first chord.

Try to play as many tunes as possible by ear—starting with simple short tunes to gain experience. However, do not be disappointed if some do not seem to work out—leave them until another day and try again.

As you will have gathered, playing by ear is a matter of taking a tune you can sing (or hear in your head), and finding the notes for it on the guitar. As long as you can hear whether you are playing the right or wrong note or chord, and have the patience to experiment a little to find the right notes or chords, you can work out many different tunes. Playing by ear is not a substitute for reading music. Most musicians use both methods for learning new music, depending on how difficult or complicated a tune is.

## PLAYING FINGERPICKING AND BRUSH STROKES BY EAR
Fingerpicking and Brush Stroke backings can be made up for many tunes after you have worked out the chords and the rhythm. Choose patterns which suit the music and have the same number of beats as the rhythm. Play the 'name' note of each chord as the main Bass Note and add extra notes and runs, to change the patterns occasionally and stop them sounding rigid or mechanical. It is best to play mainly Open Chords with Fingerpicking or Brush Stroke backings, until you become expert.

Some tunes can be made into guitar solos, like those shown in this book, by playing the melody with Fingerpicking or Brush Strokes. If you think a tune may be suitable, work out the chords and a Fingerpicking or Brush Stroke backing in the Keys of C or G, Am or Em. Then work out the melody on its own on the 3rd, 4th, 5th and 6th strings (for playing by the thumb), or on the 1st, 2nd and 3rd strings (for playing with the fingers). Next, finger the chords and try playing the melody with notes in the chords, or by taking off or adding fingers to them on different frets. If this does not work, try another Key (G instead of C) or another tune!

If the tune does work, play the melody very slowly with the chords and try fitting it to different fingerpicking or brush stroke patterns. You may need to alter the pattern or the melody slightly to keep a steady rhythm. Then gradually speed up.

Experiment with different tunes in different Keys and listen to other players to learn more about melody playing within these styles.

———

The chords to 'Jingle Bells' go C F C D7 G7, C F C G7 C with a 4 beats to the Bar rhythm.
'Happy Birthday' chords go C G7 C F G7 C with a 3 beat rhythm.

# Helpful Hints and Friendly Advice

**HAVE FUN—PLAY GUITAR WITH A FRIEND . . . . .**
You can have a lot of fun by playing with another guitarist or with a friend who sings or plays another instrument.

If you have a friend who plays the guitar, piano or organ, ask him or her to play the chords to a tune while you play the melody. Then change over and let your friend play the melody while you play the backing. If your friend sings or plays another instrument, let him or her sing or play the melody while you play a chord backing.

Choose tunes which you both know, if possible, and read the same music. It is not a good idea to attempt anything new before you have had time to practise it on your own. Make sure you are both in tune with each other before you start (see page 27). If you have problems on agreeing on the Keys in which you play, a Capo may help (see page 81), or you may want to change the music into another Key, as explained on page 106.

Count the beat before you begin, so you both start together at the same speed. To accompany singing, play the first few chords, or part of the melody as an 'Introduction' to give the singer the starting notes.

If you play backings or fingerpicking with another guitarist, a good full sound can be made if one guitar is played without a Capo, while the other is played with a Capo, with the chords 'transposed' to another Key. For example, one guitarist plays chords in C (say C, F and G7) while the other plays chords in G (say G, C and D7) with a Capo at the 5th fret.

If you do not know anyone who sings or plays, a guitar teacher, a guitar society or your music shop may be able to recommend someone.

**. . . . . OR PLAY WITH A RECORDING OF YOURSELF**
With a little practice, you can record your own backings to tunes on a cassette or tape recorder, and play melodies along with them whenever you wish. Position the microphone near the soundhole of the guitar, but not so close that you might knock into it. Switch on the recorder and count a few extra beats at the beginning so you will know where to start when you play back the tape. Play a little more slowly than usual, be careful not to speed up, and play the backing through at least twice. Then wind back the tape and play the melody along with the recorded backing.

You can also record Fingerpicking, Brush Strokes and other styles to hear whether you are playing smoothly and correctly.

## PLAYING ALONG WITH RECORDS

Playing along with records can be good practice, particularly for Lead and Rhythm Guitarists, as it is almost like being part of the group or band. However, it is not always as easy as you might think, until you learn the trick, so start with slow simple tunes which you know well.

You may need to adjust the tuning of your guitar *very slightly* to be in tune with a record. Put on the record and play different notes until you can hear whether your guitar sounds the same, or higher or lower. It should never need much adjustment, unless the guitar is out of tune with itself. Tune the guitar if necessary, then play along with the record patiently trying to fit in single notes or chords until you can play the whole tune. If you have real difficulty with one tune, try another track on the same record. It may be worthwhile buying the 'Sheet Music' for a tune you particularly like, because it is often written in the same Key as the original recording. If it is not in the same Key, try playing with a Capo behind different frets or change the music to another Key as explained on page 106.

If you like Lead or Jazz guitar playing, copy and practise some of your favourite guitarist's solos, and work out your own improvised (made-up) solos to play along with records. Look for books of Jazz, Dance-Band or Group music which give Lead Guitar solos and runs, preferably for tunes you have on record, so you can play along. Learn new chords from Jazz or Dance-Band Chord books.

## DO YOU NEED A NEW GUITAR?

Unless your guitar seems difficult to play and is limiting your playing, or it does not suit the music you like, you probably do not *really need* a new guitar. However, if you want a different type of guitar, or can afford a more expensive instrument with a better tone, you would be well advised to buy one before prices go higher. Choose a new guitar even more carefully than you would choose your first guitar, because it will cost more and you will expect it to last for many years. Make sure you follow all the advice given on pages 12-15.

Before you write off your old guitar, put on a new set of strings, and have it checked by a music shop which handles repairs. The result of a little work may surprise you. Even if you buy a new guitar, you may find your old one useful for playing other types of music, or for taking to places where you would not want to risk a new guitar. Otherwise you might consider selling it, or part - exchanging it for a new instrument.

112

## BUYING AN 'ELECTRIC' GUITAR OR AMPLIFIER

Before you buy an 'electric' guitar or an amplifier, try to speak to an experienced guitarist, preferably from a group or band which plays the kind of music which interests you, and ask for his advice.

The most important parts of an 'electric' guitar are the pick-ups, which convert the string vibrations into electrical signals for the amplifier, and the 'action' which affects how easily and quickly the left-hand fingers can play—particularly higher up the fingerboard. Choose the guitar with the best pick-ups and fastest, easiest action at a price you can afford. Compare several guitars—including more expensive instruments—and play them with the type of amplifier you intend to use. Check that all switches and controls work properly without making clicking or scraping noises through the amplifier. Make sure each pick-up gives a balanced sound— each string should sound equally loud and clear when the guitar is played with the amplifier.

Choose an amplifier which suits your kind of music and the places you play. If you are going to play loud music to large audiences, you need a powerful amplifier with speakers which can more than handle the high output. For quieter music and smaller clubs, a less powerful 'amp' may suffice, but it is best to have slightly more power than you need to avoid overloading the amplifier. Look for a good variation in tone from bright treble to mellow bass, minimum distortion and low 'hiss' or 'hum' levels at high volume. It is not worth paying extra for gimmicky effects on an amplifier unless you intend to use them. Choose well-known makes with a good guarantee and buy from a dealer who can handle any repairs or servicing *quickly*. Take plenty of time before you decide and get the help of an expert guitarist if possible.

## SELLING A GUITAR

If you have taken care of your guitar, you may be able to sell it for a good price, or part-exchange it for another instrument. Before trying to sell it, clean the guitar thoroughly and wipe over the fingerboard with a slightly damp cloth. Put on a new set of strings two weeks or so before you sell it, so the guitar will sound good but not go out of tune when someone plays it. Remember to tune your guitar before anyone comes to see it.

Advertise it on a notice board or in a newspaper, unless you have a friend who would like it, or a guitar teacher who needs an instrument for another pupil. If you are buying another guitar, your music shop may give you an idea of the price you should ask for your old one, or take it in part-exchange.

# Playing to an Audience

Sooner or later someone is going to ask you to play the guitar for them, or you are going to want to go out and share your music with other people. The same advice applies whether you play for an audience of hundreds, or just for your family and friends.

Always tune your guitar carefully in a separate room before you play for anyone. If you are going to play anywhere but in your own home, go early and take out your guitar so it can adjust itself to the temperature for a while before you tune it. This way it is less likely to go out of tune when you play it. However, do not leave it near a radiator or window. If you cannot find a quiet place to tune it, rest your right ear against the side of the guitar while adjusting the strings and you will find it easier to hear.

Choose music which you are confident to perform. Do not play the most complicated piece you know, or the most recent tune you have learned, as you are more likely to make embarrassing mistakes with these. If you are going to play more than one piece, pick tunes with different rhythms and speeds, in different Keys (or use a capo at different frets), so your music does not all sound the same. Mix loud and soft tunes and save the best and most dramatic pieces until last.

Work out good beginnings and endings for your tunes to make your playing entertaining and professional-sounding. Try to hear each tune in your head before starting to play it to get the speed and the feeling of the music right.

*Never* announce that "you cannot play very well" or "you will probably make mistakes or forget the words"—this kind of talk is likely to make you do these very things. If you do make a mistake, make a joke of it, or ignore it—most people probably will not notice. *Never* play with cold hands because your fingers will be stiff.

There are many places where you can play in public if you want to—College and Guitar Society Concerts, Local Talent Nights, Folk Clubs and other places you may find advertised in local papers, music magazines or on notice boards. Alternatively arrange musical evenings or picnics with your friends or family.

Playing to an audience, once you have conquered the initial nerves everyone has, is a good way to improve your playing because it gives you the incentive to play better and polish your music. Practise playing to an audience by looking out of a window while you play, and imagining that the whole world is watching and listening to you.

# Travelling with your guitar

Take special care of your guitar whenever you take it outside your home. Always carry it inside its case—even if you are only going a short distance—and protect it from sun or rain. If you are going to travel with it frequently, particularly by public transport, it is probably worth buying a strong 'hard' case, and insuring the guitar *and* case.

If you travel by car, lay the guitar flat on its back where it will not slide forward if the car is stopped suddenly. For this reason, it will normally be safer in the boot (trunk) rather than on the back seat. The head of the guitar should not touch anything which might knock it out of tune, or strain the neck. Never leave your guitar in a parked car all day or all night as it may be damaged by the heat, cold or damp to which it could be exposed.

On a bus or train, it is probably safest lying flat on its back on a luggage rack, as long as you can keep an eye on it, and remember it when you get off! Otherwise, hold it upright on the floor by your feet.

If you travel by 'plane, a hard case is almost essential, as most airlines do not allow guitars to be taken into the cabin. Stick 'fragile' labels all over the case and put a little loose padding around the guitar. Airlines normally take good care of 'fragile items', however you may be asked to sign a form saying they are not responsible, so insure your guitar before your trip. At the end of the flight, go quickly to the Baggage Claim Area and ask where the 'fragile items' arrive.

If you are going to another country with your guitar, take the receipt of purchase with you because you may need it for Customs.

If you are intending to play in public for money in another country, *write* to the Embassy or Consulate of that country to find out whether you must declare your guitar to their Customs, *or if you are liable to pay import duty on it as a performer*. If this is the case, you will probably be best advised to hire a guitar (and amplifier) there.

If you insure your guitar, give the insurance company the make, model and serial numbers—these are normally found on the head or inside the body of the guitar. Insure the guitar and its case on an 'All-Risks' Policy for what it would cost to replace, rather than what you paid for it, and increase its value every year.

# Changing the strings on your guitar

Put a new set of strings on your guitar every two or three months—even if it has not been played much. If you play a great deal and want to keep a good sound, you should change the strings more frequently. Old or worn strings sound dead, are more difficult to tune, make playing harder and may even strain the guitar. Change strings at the first sign of corrosion or wear. Replace all of the strings if one string breaks, because they are probably all worn. (If you replace just one of the wound strings, it will sound brighter than the others and give the guitar a peculiar sound.) However, if the 1st or 2nd string breaks when you have a fairly new set of strings on the guitar, it can usually be replaced on its own without any problem.

Be sure to buy the correct strings for your instrument. Steel strings should never be put on a guitar made for nylon strings because the instrument could be permanently damaged. Nylon strings do not suit guitars made for steel strings either—they give a poor sound and may buzz. Ask your music shop or other guitarists to recommend good quality strings, and try different makes until you find strings which suit you. Always keep a spare set of strings in your guitar case. (See page 119 for advice on different types and gauges of steel strings.)

Clean the head and fingerboard with a slightly damp cloth *before* you put on new strings. Any awkward parts can be cleaned when each string is taken off—but take care not to get the new strings wet.

## TAKE OFF ONE STRING AT A TIME
Take off one string at a time, and leave the rest tuned up, as this makes re-tuning easier. It is best to start with the 6th string—
Slacken the string until it is loose enough to pull out of the tuning machine. Then remove it from the bridge, like this—
On nylon-strung guitars, and some steel-strung guitars, the loose end of the string is pushed through its hole in the bridge or tail-piece until it comes out, or is loose enough to un-tie and pull through. On guitars with 'Pin Bridges' (see drawing on next page), push the string into the bridge, gently pull out the bridge pin, then remove the string. Do not force the pin or string—wiggle it about to loosen it. (In extreme necessity only, wrap a thick cloth around the pin and hold it in pliers while you wiggle it.)

Take the 6th string out of its packet and unwind it. Find the end which is most flexible or has a 'ball' connected to it. Strings with ball-ends are threaded through the hole in the back of the bridge or fitted into the slot on the tail-piece, except on guitars with 'Pin Bridges'.

If your guitar has a Pin Bridge, insert the string like this—
1. Push the ball-end of the string right through the hole in the bridge.
2. Insert the Pin. The string should run along the slot in the pin if there is one.
3. Press down on the pin and pull the loose end of the string tight.

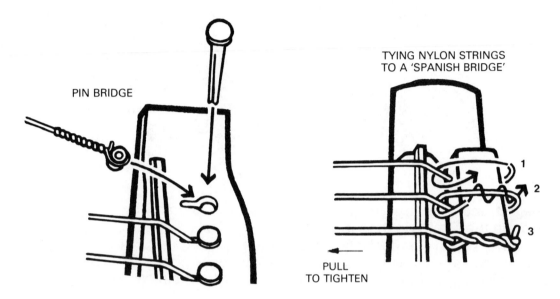

PIN BRIDGE

TYING NYLON STRINGS
TO A 'SPANISH BRIDGE'

1

2

3

PULL
TO TIGHTEN

Nylon strings without ball-ends are tied to the bridge like this—
1. Push the flexible end of the string through the hole near the bridge bone, bring it back over the bridge and loop it under and around itself (as shown in the drawing).
2. Wind the last inch or so (25mm) twice around the loop.
3. Pull the loose end of the string to tighten your winding.

When the string is attached to the bridge or tail-piece, bring it loosely up the neck and thread it through the hole in its tuning machine. Hold the string in its notch in the nut and gently turn its tuning peg until the string is no longer slack. (Ideally, the string should be slack enough when you start, to wind 2 or 3 times around the post or barrel of the tuning machine before it is in tune, to prevent slipping.)

Finger the 6th string behind the 5th fret and gently tighten it until it is in tune with the 5th string open. Then take some of the stretch out of it by pushing the middle of the string down across the other strings several times with your right thumb. Then tune it again.

Replace and 'stretch' the other strings in the same way. Then tune the 1st string to your pitch pipe or tuning fork and check the tuning again.

Always make sure each string is attached to the correct tuning machine and wound in the right direction. Each string goes over and around the barrel on 'Spanish' type guitar heads. On other guitar heads, each string goes up the middle and around the top of its post.

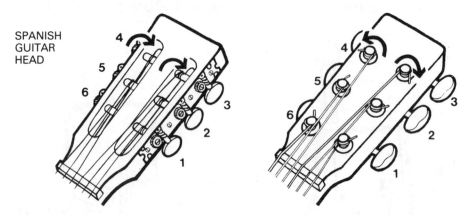

SPANISH GUITAR HEAD

The 1st and 2nd strings can be stopped from slipping by putting them through their holes in the tuning machines twice. (Push the string through the hole, round the post and through the hole again.) Cut off the loose end of each steel string with wire cutters to leave about ½" (12mm). This keeps the head of the guitar tidy and removes a main cause of annoying rattling and buzzing noises.

Nylon strings can be left long, if you wish. Then, if a string breaks, there may be enough of it left to put back on the guitar as a very temporary spare. With nylon strings, the guitar will be easier to keep in tune if you put on the 4th, 5th and 6th strings first and let them stretch out for a few days, before putting on the other three strings.

New strings always go out of tune when they are first put on a guitar. If possible, leave them overnight to settle down, and tune them again before you play your guitar for anyone. Otherwise, you are likely to spend more time tuning than playing.

Keep your used strings, unless they are old or badly worn, because they can make useful spares. Wash used nylon strings in warm, soapy water and rinse them clean. Steel strings can be boiled in a pan of water to clean them. When the strings are dry, roll them up like new strings. Identify each different string and put it in the packet which belonged to the matching new string. Keep these strings in your guitar case, to use as temporary spares if a string breaks while you are out playing—if you put on one new string when you are playing, it will not match the sound of the other strings, and will keep going out of tune.

# Choosing your Steel Guitar Strings

Steel strings are made with various windings in several gauges to suit different styles of playing. For general acoustic playing, medium or light gauge bronze-wound strings with a wound 3rd string are preferred by the author, but make your own choice with the help of the guide given here, depending on your kind of music and the sound you prefer.

*Heavy Gauge*—For heavy rhythm playing and chunky chords. Heavy gauge strings are only suitable for very strong guitars—and strong fingers.

*Medium Gauge*—Good all-round mellow sounding strings which last well for fingerpicking and playing with a plectrum.

*Light Gauge*—Good for fingerpicking, light plectrum playing, blues, and so on. These strings are fairly fast for lead playing and give bright sounding chords. However, they do not give as much 'Bass' as medium gauge and may not last as long.

*Extra-Light Gauge*—These strings are usually too light for most acoustic guitars, and may buzz. They are good for fast 'electric' lead playing and for 'bending' notes.

*Ultra-Light Gauge*—Made for very fast 'electric' lead guitar playing, these strings give long sustained notes and 'bend' very easily. However, Ultra-Light strings are far too light for many guitars.

*IMPORTANT!* Use a *wound* 3rd steel string for general playing. Unwound 3rd strings may give odd sounding chords, and are normally used only for special lead or blues effects.

BRONZE-WOUND steel strings are recommended for a good ringing acoustic sound, but are not really suitable for 'electric' playing.

FLAT-WOUND and GROUND-WOUND strings are for 'electric' guitars only. They give a smooth slick sound, and allow the fingers to slide silently along the strings. However, they feel heavier than regular wound strings, and are not as good for long sustained notes and 'controlled feed-back' effects.

# How to play Harmonics

'Harmonics', 'bell-tones' or 'chimes' are high notes used for special effects and as an aid to tuning. They can be played on all the strings in several places, but the clearest, most useful harmonics are those found directly over the 12th, 7th, and 5th frets.

The easiest harmonics to play are over the 12th fret—
1. Rest your left-hand 2nd finger lightly on the 6th string directly over the 12th fret. The finger should touch the string but not press it.

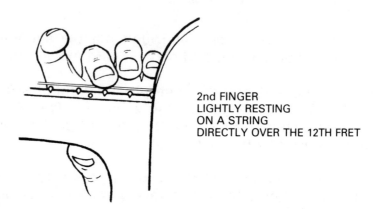

2nd FINGER
LIGHTLY RESTING
ON A STRING
DIRECTLY OVER THE 12TH FRET

2. Pluck the 6th string firmly, then remove the left-hand finger. A long clear bell-like note should sound.

Practise playing harmonics on all the strings over the 12th fret. When you can make clear bell-like notes there, try playing the harmonics over the 7th and 5th frets in the same way. These are not as strong, but you should be able to play them with a little practice.

Parts of some melodies can be played with the harmonics over the 12th, 7th and 5th frets mixed together, or over just one of the frets at a time. Try a 'Bugle Call' with the harmonics over the 12th fret by playing the strings in this order—4  3  3  2  3  4,  4  3  3  2  3.

Harmonic chords can be played by lightly resting the 1st finger across several of the strings, like a 'Barré' or 'Half-Barré'—
The 1st, 2nd and 3rd string harmonics make an Em Chord over the 12th and 5th frets, and a Bm Chord over the 7th fret.
The 1st, 2nd, 3rd and 4th string harmonics make a G6 Chord over the 12th and 5th frets, and a D6 Chord over the 7th fret.
These chords can be used to finish tunes. Try G6 over the 12th fret, D6 over the 7th fret, then G6 over the 5th fret, to end a tune in G.

## HARMONICS—THEIR POSITIONS AND NOTE NAMES

(DOTTED LINES JOIN NOTES WHICH ARE THE SAME)

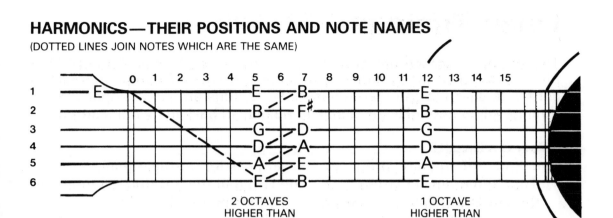

2 OCTAVES
HIGHER THAN
OPEN STRINGS

1 OCTAVE
HIGHER THAN
OPEN STRINGS
(SAME NOTES AS STRINGS)
PLAYED BEHIND 12th FRET)

## How to tune with Harmonics

When you have learned to play clear, long-sounding harmonics, you can use them to tune your guitar very accurately, even in comparatively noisy situations. The following methods of tuning work very well—

1. Tune the 1st string to a tuning fork, or to another instrument.
2. Play the 2nd string 12th fret harmonic and compare it with the normal fretted note on the 1st string behind the 7th fret, *OR* compare the 2nd string 5th fret harmonic with the 1st string 7th fret harmonic. Adjust the 2nd string until both notes sound the same.
3. Compare the 3rd string 12th fret harmonic with the note on the 1st string behind the 3rd fret, and adjust the 3rd string.
4. Compare the 4th string 12th fret harmonic with the note on the 2nd string behind the 3rd fret, and adjust the 4th string.
5. Compare the 5th string 12th fret harmonic with the note on the 3rd string behind the 2nd fret, *OR* (better), compare 5th string 5th fret harmonic with the 4th string 7th fret harmonic, *OR* compare the 5th string 7th fret harmonic with the 1st string open, and adjust the 5th string.
6. Compare the 6th string 12th fret harmonic with the note on the 4th string behind the 2nd fret, *OR* compare the 6th string 5th fret harmonic with the 5th string 7th fret harmonic, *OR* compare the 6th string 5th fret harmonic with the 1st string open. Adjust the 6th string until both notes sound the same.

Let the harmonics ring while you are adjusting the strings, because you can often hear them move into tune. In noisy places, rest your right ear against the side of the guitar to hear better. Try all of these methods and choose the one which suits you best.

# Open Tunings

The guitar is sometimes tuned differently in Blues and Fingerpicking playing. Most of these different tunings are 'Open Tunings' in which a complete chord is sounded when all the strings are played open. These tunings allow melodies and solos to be played backed by open strings.

### OPEN G TUNING
The 2nd, 3rd and 4th strings are the same as for normal tuning.
1. Tune the open 1st string to the 2nd string at the 3rd fret, *OR* tune it to the 4th string 12th fret harmonic, giving the note D.
2. Press the 6th string behind the 7th fret and tune it to the 5th string open, *OR* tune the 6th string 12th fret harmonic to the 4th string open, giving the note D.
3. Press the 5th string behind the 7th fret, and tune it to the 4th string open, *OR* tune the 5th string 12 fret harmonic to the 3rd string open, giving the note G.

### OPEN D TUNING
The 4th and 5th strings are the same as for normal tuning.
1. Tune the open 1st string to D, as explained for Open G Tuning.
2. Tune the 2nd string open to the 3rd string at the 2nd fret, *OR* tune it to the 5th string 12th fret harmonic, giving the note A.
3. Tune the 3rd string to the 4th string at the 4th fret, giving F♯.
4. Tune the open 6th string to D as explained for Open G Tuning.

Normal chord shapes do not work in Open Tunings—
In Open G Tuning, a 1st finger Barré across all the strings makes a C Chord at the 5th fret, a D Chord at the 7th fret, and so on.
In Open D Tuning, a 1st finger Barré across all the strings makes a G Chord at the 5th fret, an A Chord at the 7th fret, and so on.
Some other chord shapes are shown here—

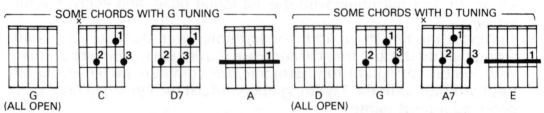

When you have finished playing, re-tune your guitar by working up and down from the 4th string—it does not change in either tuning.

WARNING! Avoid tunings which *raise* the pitch of the strings because the guitar may be damaged—Use Open D tuning instead of Open E Tuning.

# The Problem Page

Most problems which occur with guitars are small ones which can easily be fixed, so before worrying that something is seriously wrong, see if you can find a remedy here. If you cannot solve the problem, or if your guitar has become difficult to play, ask for the advice of an experienced guitarist, a guitar repairer or music shop.

### BUZZING AND RATTLING NOISES
1. If the guitar rattles, turn it face down and shake it so anything which may have fallen inside will drop out of the soundhole.
2. If it buzzes, check that the loose end of a string is not vibrating against the tuning machines, and bend any loose ends out of the way.
3. If any of the wound strings buzz or sound dead, the winding may be broken, in which case replace all of the strings.
4. If most of the strings buzz, the guitar may be tuned too low or a slightly heavier set of strings may be needed. Alternatively, the bridge may be too low—If it is adjustable, turn the screws a little to raise it slightly. Never tune a guitar higher to eliminate string buzzing as this could cause serious damage.

### IF STRINGS KEEP BREAKING
1. Make sure you are not playing too hard, or tuning the guitar too high. (Check the tuning with a pitch pipe or tuning fork.)
2. If a string keeps breaking in the same place, there may be a sharp edge on the nut, tuning machine, frets or bridge—see a repairer.

### PROBLEMS WITH TUNING, OR STAYING IN TUNE
1. If the guitar keeps going out of tune while you are playing, you may be playing too hard, or tuning and playing it before it has reached room temperature, or new strings may need 'stretching'—see page 117.
2. If the guitar is in tune at the lower frets, but seems out of tune when played higher up the neck, the bridge may be in the wrong position. Check this by measuring from the nut to the 12th fret. This should be the same as the distance from the 12th fret to the bridge bone. If the bridge is of the moveable type, move it to the correct position.
   If the guitar is out of tune with a Capo, check that the Capo is parallel to the frets. Use a curved Capo on a curved fingerboard.

Tuning problems and buzzing may also be caused by raised or badly worn frets or a warped or twisted neck—all problems for a guitar repairer.

Any electrical problems with an 'electric' guitar or amplifier are best dealt with by the dealer who supplied them or an amplifier specialist.

# Are you Left-Handed?

Many left-handed people have no problem learning to play the guitar in the usual way. In fact, they often learn more quickly, because the left hand does the most intricate work in the first part of guitar playing. However, the regular guitar does not suit everyone who is left-handed, so before you buy a guitar, it is best to find out whether you can play the regular instrument, or if you need a special left-handed guitar.

If you can, borrow a guitar from a friend, or hire one from a music or hire shop for a few weeks.

Hold the guitar and start to play as explained in pages 17 to 26. If it feels *completely* wrong and un-natural, turn the guitar around and try playing the other way. If this is *much* easier, look for a left-handed guitar, or a guitar which can be easily converted for you to play left-handed. If you find no real difference between left- and right-handed playing, learn to play the usual way and avoid the need for a special guitar.

If you decide to play a left-handed guitar, you can learn with this and other books by using your right hand when the book says 'left hand', and vice versa. None of the music will need changing, but all diagrams and drawings will be wrong for you, because the strings are put on the other way around. Trace each diagram or drawing, then turn it over to see how it should appear for left-handed playing. Put your tracings in a book so you can refer to them. The diagrams for the first notes and chords are given here to help you start. Good luck with your playing.

SOME NOTES ON LEFT-HANDED GUITARS

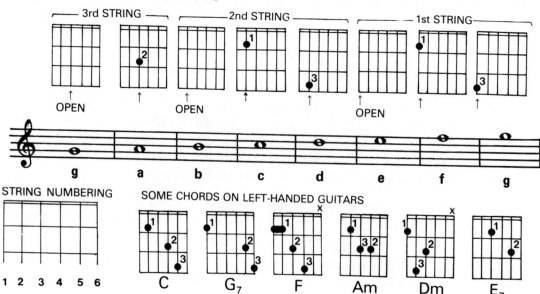